AN

UNCOMMON

GUIDE

TO

Florida

A Resident's Guide to the Real Florida

Other Books by Nina McGuire and Barbara Budd:

An Uncommon Guide to Minnesota

An Uncommon Guide to the Twin Cities

An Uncommon Dining Guide to the Twin Cities

Cover Design:
Success by Design, Inc.
Cover Photograph:
Florida Department of Tourism,
Cypress Gardens

AN

UNCOMMON

GUIDE

TO

Florida

A glove compartment companion for
residents, newcomers, and tourists.
Special things to do and see for all age groups.
Over 1,000 activities to help you explore the state's past,
present, and future. Take the uncommon tours and ...
Florida will never look the same!

By Nina McGuire

Tailored Tours Publications

First Edition

Printed and bound in the United States of America by Rose Printing Company, Inc., Tallahassee, FL.

ISBN: 0-9631241-0-2

Library of Congress Catalog Card Number: 91-66907

Welcome

Welcome to my Florida, a land of uncommon contrasts. The state's story is peopled with brilliant entrepreneurs, imaginative dreamers, and empire builders. These are the architects, town planners, artists, authors, composers, sports heroes, showmen, scoundrels, and "just plain folks" who created Florida. You'll meet them all in this book.

Each of the 24 uncommon tours can be accomplished in a few days. However, it is easily possible to spend weeks in each of the major areas described. Your time and budget considerations are the limiting factors. The tours have been grouped for easy driving. All admission prices have been noted and are current as of late 1991. As you will see, many of the most interesting things to do and see are free.

One of the aims of the book has been to help the traveller stay off tollroads and interstates. There is no negative implied in this statement. In urging you to travel the state's scenic byways, it is expected that you will discover many of your own personal, uncommon glimpses of our state. The back roads help you develop impressions of how the 20th century has settled on land where prehistoric animals once roamed, where the country's oldest bald cypress tree took root 3,500 years ago, and where Indian nations made their homes. These routes take you to plantations, Civil War sites, attractions, and pristine beaches.

It is fitting that The Greatest Show on Earth begins in Florida each year. Welcome! Come along, take the uncommon tours, and enjoy Florida!

Acknowledgments

First, I would like to thank the many friends who have so willingly shared their knowledge and love of their favorite Florida adventures. They have been generous with their time, energy, experience, and suggestions.

Without the following state and federal organizations, this book could not have been written. Their cooperation, research facilities, and encouragement made all the difference.

The Florida State Archives
The Florida Department of Natural Resources
The Florida Department of State
The Florida Department of Transportation
The Florida Department of Tourism, and
The U.S. National Park Service

Three people provided invaluable guidance in the selection of the photography used in this book. They are Dixie Lee Nims of the Florida Department of Tourism and Joan Miller and Joanna Norman of the Florida Photography Archives. Their thoughtful comments, suggestions, and guidance have added richness to the book. I am grateful to them.

During the researching of this book, many Chamber of Commerce and Economic Development people throughout the state have offered suggestions and advice. Without exception, they have been helpful in providing information and materials about their specific areas of the state. The same comment applies to librarians and booksellers who shared their insights and guided the development of the book as you see it today.

Although no one at any of the sites referenced knew that a book was being researched, I would like to thank the many people who share their knowledge, excitement, and love of Florida. These people staff our parks, museums, and other facilities referenced in the book. Their joy in helping us understand the wealth of wonderful experiences in Florida's past, present, and future is contagious.

Florida's pioneer families came by boat, wagon train, and railroad to make Florida their home. They created towns, schools, and political processes. Their contributions and hardships are recognized.

The early tourists came by stagecoach, steamboat, railroad, and automobile to enjoy the state. In the early 20th century, so many came by car that they became known as the "tin can tourists." They are thanked.

Although many have helped, the final book is my responsibility alone. No gratuities or other considerations have been received from any of the establishments mentioned. My criteria was to select those facilities which to me were outstanding, unique, and worth sharing with you.

Particular thanks is offered to Sara, Doug, Stuart, and Michele. These members of my family provided invaluable assistance and support throughout all the stages of the development of this Uncommon Guide.

My hope is that this small paperback book will find a place in your glove compartment as you tour Florida and create your own adventures and memories.

Tin Can Tourists, Tampa, Christmas Day, 1920

Table
of
Contents

Welcome, 5

Acknowledgments, 6

The Uncommon Tours, 10

Northeastern Florida, 12

Tour 1. The Buccaneer's Trail, 13
Tour 2. America's Oldest Settlement, 21

East Central Florida, 31

Tour 3. Millionaires, Sand, and Auto Speed Records, 33
Tour 4. The Space Frontier, 37
Tour 5. Lighthouse Row, 49

Southeastern Florida, 53

Tour 6. The Gold Coast, 55
Tour 7. The Miami Seven, 65
Tour 8. River of Grass, 77
Tour 9. Hemingway's Haunts, 83

Central Florida, 94

Tour 10. Orlando and the Citrus Rim, 95
Tour 11. The Tourist's Mecca, 101
Tour 12. Hill Country Adventures, 111

West Coast Florida, 116

Tour 13. The Dynamic Duo, 117
Tour 14. Greatest Show on Earth, 125
Tour 15. Time–Lapse Territory, 141

Continued

The Uncommon Tours, continued

Gulf Coast Florida, 148

Tour 16. The Start of Statehood, 149
Tour 17. Extraordinary Beaches, 155
Tour 18. Pensacola, City of Five Flags, 161

Northern Panhandle, 165

Tour 19. The Spanish Explorer's Trail, 166
Tour 20. The Capitol Connection, 171
Tour 21. Canopy Roads and Indian Springs, 175
Tour 22. The Tobacco Road, 181

North Central Florida, 185

Tour 23. A Composer and the Suwannee River, 187
Tour 24. Thoroughbreds All, 190

Annual Events, 198

Index, 208

Photographic Credits, 222

After Words, 223

Gone Touring...
Panhandle Beaches

The Uncommon Tours

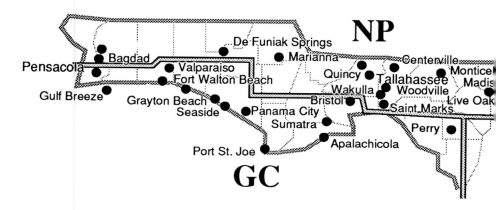

Florida is a wonderful state to explore! The book has been divided into eight major areas.

Northeastern Florida (NE)
East Central Florida (EC)
Southeastern Florida (SE)
Central Florida (C)
West Coast Florida (WC)
Gulf Coast Florida (GC)
Northern Panhandle (NP)
North Central Florida (NC)

Although each of the tours in the book is self–contained, the book has been designed so that most tours link with tours in connecting areas. The maps outlined in the book are provided as general reference points. Two maps which are particularly useful as armchair and auto companions are *Florida's Official Transportation Map* which is distributed through the State's Department of Commerce and the detailed *Florida Atlas & Gazetteer* which is available in many bookstores.

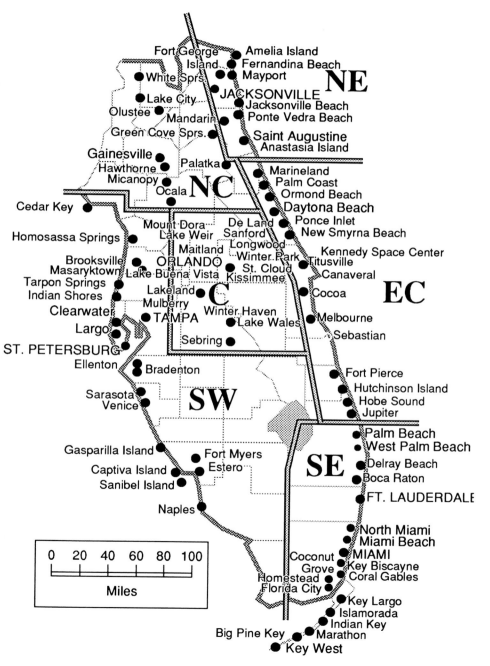

Fort George Island
Amelia Island
Fernandina Beach
Mayport
White Sprs.
NE
Lake City
JACKSONVILLE
Olustee
Jacksonville Beach
Mandarin
Ponte Vedra Beach
Green Cove Sprs.
Saint Augustine
Anastasia Island
Gainesville
Palatka
Hawthorne
Marineland
Micanopy
Palm Coast
Ocala
NC
Ormond Beach
Cedar Key
Daytona Beach
Mount Dora
De Land
Ponce Inlet
Homosassa Springs
Lake Weir
Sanford
New Smyrna Beach
Longwood
Maitland
Kennedy Space Center
Winter Park
Brooksville
ORLANDO
Titusville
Masaryktown
Lake Buena Vista
St. Cloud
Tarpon Springs
Kissimmee
Canaveral
Indian Shores
Lakeland
Cocoa
EC
Clearwater
Mulberry
C
Winter Haven
Largo
TAMPA
Lake Wales
Melbourne
ST. PETERSBURG
Sebring
Sebastian
Ellenton
Bradenton
Fort Pierce
Hutchinson Island
SW
Sarasota
Hobe Sound
Venice
Jupiter
Palm Beach
Gasparilla Island
West Palm Beach
Fort Myers
Captiva Island
Estero
SE
Delray Beach
Sanibel Island
Boca Raton
FT. LAUDERDALE
Naples
North Miami
Miami Beach
Coconut
MIAMI
Grove
Key Biscayne
Homestead
Coral Gables
Florida City
Key Largo
Islamorada
Indian Key
Big Pine Key
Marathon
Key West

0 20 40 60 80 100

Miles

Northeastern Florida

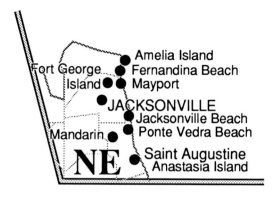

Northeastern Florida provides a beautiful study in contrasts. In a short distance the traveller moves from some of the quietest beaches in the state, to the oldest city in the nation, and then on to the largest land mass city in the continental U.S. Two tour routes are highlighted for your enjoyment.

The Buccaneer's Trail begins on Amelia Island and travels south through Fernandina Beach, once one of the state's wealthiest communities. It crosses barrier islands and beautiful beaches before turning inland along the St. Johns River. While travelling west, there is a stop at the state's oldest plantation, a brief ferry ride to climb aboard a state–of–the–art naval vessel, a trip to the zoo, and a visit to the fascinating city of Jacksonville.

St. Augustine is *America's Oldest Settlement.* The historic city has been caringly restored. Skilled rangers and guides throughout the Old City introduce you to Florida's settlement–as it was 400 years ago.

The return trip to Jacksonville ambles along the St. Johns River where steamboats travelled. Stop in Mandarin, the town where Harriett Beecher Stowe wrote of the post–Civil War period.

Amelia Island
Fort George
Island
Fernandina Beach
Mayport
JACKSONVILLE

Tour 1.
The
Buccaneer's
Trail

Amelia Island – Fernandina Beach

As the state's northernmost island, Amelia Island became a safe haven for smugglers and pirates during the pre–Civil War days. The pirates would outrun Federal gunboats and land safely in the Florida Territory.

During the Victorian period, the Island became the Easternmost terminus for the state's first cross–state railroad. The combination of railroading and shipping made Amelia Island and Fernandina Beach desirable places to live. As you visit today, enjoy imagining life in the 19th century as you travel through the Centre Street Restoration area.

No one wanted to give up control of the Island. There were continuing feuds between buccaneers, settlers, and the U.S. Military. One way to understand these arguments is to explore *Fort Clinch State Park*. This never–finished pre–Civil War Fort was started in 1847 as part of the coastal defense network to reduce the number of smugglers carrying goods to Confederate troops. The Fort was used during the Civil War and for training U.S. Troops during the Spanish–American War.

Early drawing of Fort Clinch, Amelia Island

Plan to visit during the first weekend of any month to experience a colorful, authentic reenactment of the Fort's 1864 occupation.

Location:	2601 Atlantic Avenue
Hours:	**Park**: Daily 8–sunset. **Fort**: 9–5
Fees:	$3.25 per car, maximum of 8 people per car
Phone:	(904) 261–4212

It's only a short drive along Route 105A from the Fort to Old Fernandina.

Stop at *The Museum of History* for a capsule view of the island's rich history. Of particular interest is the 17th century Spanish Mission display and the exhibit describing the Island's plantation life. There is also a section devoted to how railroading changed the island during the Victorian era. The museum shares the island's history through the use of archaeology, photography, architecture, 19th century journalism, guides, and exhibits.

Besides the on–site facility, the museum also sponsors three walking tours through various parts of the community. The guides share interesting information about how history and the lives of residents intertwine. It's suggested that you bring your camera and wear comfortable walking shoes.

Location:	233 South 3rd Street
Hours:	**Museum Tours:** Monday through Saturday, 11 and 2. **Walking Tours:** Starting points vary, de–pending upon the tour
Fees:	**Museum:** Adults $2, students $1. **Walking Tours: Centre Tour:** Adults $5, students $4; **North and South Tours:** Adults $8 for each tour, students $4 for each tour
Phone:	(904) 261–7378. Make reservations for the walking tours at least 24 hours before your visit

The water glows, the sun and clouds signal the end of day, and the fleet floats home on a shimmering sea. Stop at the **Shrimp Docks** shortly before sunset and enjoy this sight.

Location:	Foot of Centre Street

The drive along the Buccaneer's Trail continues. The route along A1A and Route 105 between Fernandina Beach and Fort George Island is one of the most scenic in the State. It is an area of natural beauty where magnificent beaches and barrier islands make it easy to enjoy solitude and majestic views. Travel slowly enough to allow time for lunch or a stay at the elegant *Amelia Island Plantation* or pause for a swim and picnic at *Little Talbot Island State Park.*

Amelia Island Plantation

Fort George Island

If you had come from the Carolinas and Georgia in the first half of the 1800s and wanted to grow Sea Island Cotton, it would be hard to find a better location than the *Kingsley Plantation State Historic Site.* The land was good, the climate was good, and the water access was exceptional. Zephaniah Kingsley bought the plantation in 1817 for $7,000.

The homestead, Florida's oldest plantation house, has been restored. To the rear of the main house is a two story kitchen house. South of the kitchen house is the stable and nearby are the slave quarters, where over 100 slaves lived. The guided tour of the plantation house and grounds is recommended, particularly for the perspective it provides on the pre– and post– Civil War periods.

Location: 11676 Palmetto Avenue
Hours: **Grounds:** Daily 8–sunset.**Tours:** Thursday
                 through Monday at 9:30, 11, 1:30, and 3
Fees: Adults $2
Phone: (904) 251–3122

It's just a short trip from Fort George Island along Route 105 West to the *Mayport Ferry*. Take your car and enjoy a brief cruise on the St. Johns River!

Location: Highway 105 West of Fort George Island, A1A
                    at Mayport
Fee (one way):   Car $2.50, person 50¢

Mayport

Mayport is one of the oldest fishing communities in the United States, dating back over 300 years. Although fishing is still very important to the community, the Naval Station and the overall growth of the Jacksonville area have also had a major impact on the town.

All up and down the East Coast, lighthouses and houses of refuge were built to provide early warnings and safe havens for mariners in distress. *St. Johns Lighthouse* is the first of several interesting and different lighthouse stops we'll make along the Atlantic Coast. Although lighthouses in this area were built as early as the 1850s, this lighthouse dates from 1954. The seaward views are terrific and the glimpses of the Naval Station are interesting.

A weekend visit to the *Mayport Naval Station* is special! Tour one of our country's major aircraft carriers and perhaps have the opportunity to talk with one of the sailors who served during the Persian Gulf Crisis. Depending upon which vessels are in port, you may be able to tour the *USS Saratoga*, the *USS Forrestal*, or one of many other carriers for which Mayport is home port. Phone ahead for details concerning which carrier will be docked and available for touring when you're planning your visit.

Location: Check in at Naval Station Security
              Building on Mayport Road
Hours: **Lighthouse:** Saturday 10–4, Sunday 1–4. **Carrier Tours:** generally on Saturday 10–4:30, Sunday 1–4:30
Fees: No charge
Phone: **Lighthouse:** (904) 241–8845, **Naval Station:** (904) 270–5226

Although there are several ways to return to Jacksonville, it is suggested that you reboard the ferry and continue along the Buccaneer's Trail (Route 105 West).

Jacksonville

Jacksonville began as a cow crossing in 1822 and is now a major metropolitan center. The community keeps growing. At last count, Jacksonville covered over 800 square miles and was the largest land area city in the lower 48 states.

The Jacksonville Zoo houses more than 800 animals on over 60 acres. Begin your visit with a safari train tour. Kids love the elephant rides and the wonderful chimpanzee exhibit. Give them plenty of time to plan their own adventures as you travel to the African Veldt. Who knows when they'll next meet a Great White Rhino?

Location: 8605 Zoo Road
Hours: Daily 9–5, closed Thanksgiving, Christmas, and New Year's Day
Fees: Adults $4, seniors (over 65) $3, children 3–12 $2.50
Phone: (904) 757–4466

Once downtown, take a moment to stop at one of the major hotels or the Chamber of Commerce for maps and detailed information about seasonal special events. Then enjoy a leisurely walk in the downtown area to admire the architecture, both old and new. Take an elevator ride to the top of one of the tallest buildings for a bird's–eye view of the bridges that link various parts of the Jacksonville area.

If you have a day free, plan a stop at the **Farmer's Market** early in the morning, take a walk along the downtown pierside shopping area in the early evening, and simply explore this city of neighborhoods, historic districts, and ethnic areas.

The formal portion of the Jacksonville tour continues with another child–oriented activity. *The Museum of Science and History* has three floors of scientific, historical, and anthropological exhibits. There are hands–on activities, a marine aquarium, and a state–of–the–art planetarium. The two newest exhibits are *KIDSPACE*, a play–with–me introduction to science designed for children up to 48" tall. Each little one is welcome to bring an adult along to help explore the exhibit.

A second new exhibit at the Museum of Science and History is particularly relevant in Jacksonville. *Bridges, Bridges, Bridges* presents the magic, mystery, and reality of bridge construction. Also be sure to see *Sky over Jacksonville*, a free star show presented once a month (phone the Museum for details).

Location:	1025 Gulf Life Drive
Hours:	Monday through Friday 10–5, Friday and Saturday 10–6, Sunday 1–6, closed Thanksgiving, Christmas, and New Year's Day
Fees:	Adults $5, seniors (over 65), active duty military personnel, and children 4–12 $3.
Phone:	(904) 396–7062, extension 3

Jacksonville prides itself on being a working class town so it is no surprise that there is a brewery here. But, what a brewery! The gigantic *Anheuser–Busch Brewery* covers 850 acres and produces over seven million barrels of beer a year. During this one–hour tour visitors see all the processes used in the facility (note that waste water from the manufacturing process is recycled and used at the Brewery's sod farm).

You might want to plan this visit for an afternoon, choose a designated driver, and enjoy the tasting session after the tour.

Location:	111 Busch Drive
Hours:	**May through October:** Monday through Saturday 10–5. **November through March:** Monday through Saturday 9–4, closed holidays
Fees:	No charge
Phone:	(904) 751–8116

The *Cummer Gallery of Art* houses the Wark Collection of Early Meissen porcelain, fine European and American art , and Japanese Netsuke. Another major reason to visit this gallery is its two–acre, formal, waterfront garden modeled after an Italian period garden. The display in the garden changes seasonally and provides a refreshing pause before, during, or after a visit to the museum.

Location:	829 Riverside
Hours:	Tuesday through Friday 10–4, Saturday 12–5, Sunday 2–5, closed major holidays and 2 weeks in April
Fees:	No charge
Phone:	(904) 356–6857

Jacksonville's Art Museum features an excellent pre–Columbian gallery.

Location:	4160 Boulevard Center Drive
Hours:	Tuesday, Wednesday and Friday 10–4, Thursday 10–10, Saturday and Sunday 1–5, closed Thanksgiving, Christmas and New Year's Day
Fees:	No charge
Phone:	(904) 398–8336

Through the use of photographs from the State of Florida's Archives, we are able to share some examples of how the state used to look.

Before railroading largely replaced steamboats, side–wheelers such as the one pictured below travelled the St. Johns River. The steamboats carried residents and vacationing Northern-ers inland to resort communities and their bubbling springs and spas along the river's route.

One can only imagine what it must have been like to sit on the riverbank, listening to a Stephen Foster melody sliding across the water. A steamboat like the one pictured below might have rounded the bend.

*The sidewheeler, **City of Jacksonville**,*
departs from the Port of Jacksonville,
bound down the St. Johns River.
January 29, 1912

Tour 2. America's Oldest Settlement

Tour 2 combines beaches, history, and theater. The highlight of the tour is St. Augustine which is America's oldest, continuous settlement.

Jacksonville Beach

The *American Lighthouse Museum* houses a collection of paintings, scale models, photographs, architectural drawings, and navigational aids. When touring the museum, it's easy to sense how dependent yesterday's sailors were upon the lighthouses and their keepers.

Location: 1011 North 3rd Street
Hours: Tuesday through Saturday 10–5
Fees: Adults $1
Phone: (904) 241–8845

Ponte Vedra Beach

Although not well publicized, there are some fine public beaches along a 20–mile stretch of oceanfront between Ponte Vedra Beach and South Ponte Vedra Beach.

The area has had an interesting history. In 1916, two young chemical engineers sailed along the Coast looking for mineral–rich deposits. They came ashore at five– to ten–mile intervals between Brunswick, Georgia and Cape Canaveral, Florida to remove samples of beach sand. When their analysis was completed, the Ponte Vedra sand was judged to be best and a mineral processing plant was built.

During World War II, the Federal Government took over the plant and produced ilmenite and rutile, minerals that were used in the manufacture of munitions. Not surprisingly, the plant came to the attention of German military officers.

On June 16, 1942, a German submarine quietly surfaced off Ponte Vedra's shore. Four German soldiers were put into a rubber boat and rowed ashore. Beginning with the Ponte Vedra plant, they were to blow up several American defense plants. The men were seen, captured, tried, and found guilty. The plant continued production.

After the War, the plant and other properties were purchased by National Lead Company. Mining continued in the area until the State finally obtained an injunction and halted operations on the grounds that the beach, a public way, was being destroyed.

Ponte Vedra Lodge was built in 1927 to house plant employees. It has a Northland character and now serves as the centerpiece of a beach, tennis, and golf resort. Although not inexpensive, this is a wonderful spot to spend a few days—or a few weeks. Bring a bike and a bathing suit and explore!

Location:	200 Ponte Vedra Boulevard
Phone:	(904) 285–1111

St. Augustine

St. Augustine is over 400 years old and is one of America's major historic and architectural treasures. My suggestion would be for you to wear comfortable shoes and park your car anywhere in the Old City. Begin by taking a leisurely walk to explore the area. When you've done that, you may want to continue the visit with a guided tram or horse–drawn carriage ride.

St. Augustine was founded in 1565. Spanish soldiers and their families struggled to survive in this isolated outpost. They built a wooden fort which protected them for a little over a hundred years. However, it was of no value when in 1668, pirates swooped down, sacked the town, and killed 60 settlers. The surviving settlers decided to built a much stronger Fort. They constructed the *Castillo de San Marcos.*

The Castillo (or Fort) was built using then unproven building techniques and a then unknown local building material, coquina stone. Constructed between 1672 and 1695, it has never been conquered—although at various points in history it has been occupied by Spanish, British, and U.S. Military forces. Many believe its invulnerability is due to the unique, thick–walled architectural style and the use of coquina stone quarried nearby. After the Castillo was completed in 1695, no pirates ever bothered the colony again.

National Park Rangers talk of the Fort's importance and tell tales of the struggles between the seven major adversaries who tried to control St. Augustine (Spain, France, England, American Indians, as well as American Revolutionaries, Confederates, and Northerners). As you walk through the fortress, realize that it has been in constant use for more than 300 years.

As European explorers and treasure ships sailed homeward from the Western Hemisphere, the captains made use of the Gulf Stream current along St. Augustine's coast. The strategic location put the colony in the middle of continual power struggles and two wars as English and Spanish forces fought over St. Augustine and its harbor. One siege lasted six weeks, the second lasted two months. During these periods, all of the area's settlers came to live in the open courtyard inside the Fort. Imagine over 1,000 soldiers, and townsmen, women and children camping out in an area with no living quarters and only rudimentary cooking facilities.

When Havana fell to British forces in 1762, Spain, which held Cuba, decided that Cuba was more important than Florida. And so they traded Florida to Britain in return for Cuba. The resident military group changed and the Castillo was renamed the *Castle St. Mark.* British soldiers were based at the Fort to maintain control of Florida during the Revolutionary War.

After the American Revolution, in 1783, Britain gave Florida back to Spain. As the U.S. grew, diplomats worked out a treaty with Spain and acquired Florida in 1821. More and more settlers moved to the territory and tension increased between the settlers and the Seminole Indians. Here and in other parts of the Florida territory this led to three devastating wars.

Portrait of Osceola, painted from life by George Catlin. This was done at Ft. Moultrie, S.C. where Osceola was imprisioned and died a few months later in January 1838.

One of the most important leaders of the Seminoles was Osceola. He was not a chief, rather he was a spiritual leader. In October 1835, U.S. Army troops managed to capture Osceola and 300 Seminoles. They were overcome south of St. Augustine while travelling under a white flag of truce. The captives spent six weeks imprisoned at the Fort until, on November 29, 1835, 20 Indians slipped away and sucessfully escaped to the Everglades.

The scandal from this escape prompted U.S. Army officers to take Osceola North to Ft. Moultrie in Charleston, South Carolina, where he soon died. The Seminoles remaining in the Fort were shipped West to Indian territory in what is now the state of Oklahoma.

Just before President Abraham Lincoln was elected, Florida militia troops took over the Fort. Cannons were hauled away to defend Jacksonville and the St. Johns River against Union gunboats. There was no fighting here during the Civil War, even though both Confederate and Federal soldiers used the fortress. After the Civil War, Indians from the Great Plains and the Southwest were held by the U.S. Army inside the Fort. Captain Richard

Pratt tried to give these captives an education instead of punishment. His efforts led to new Indian policies and the eventual establishment of the Carlisle Indian School in Carlisle, Pennsylvania. In 1924 the Castillo was declared a National Monument and the National Park Service was assigned its care in 1933.

Location:	One Castillo Drive East
Hours:	Labor Day through Memorial Day 8:30–7:30, winter hours 9–4:45
Fees:	Adults $1, no charge for seniors (over 65) and children under 16
Phone:	(904) 829–6506

One of the best ways to begin or end a visit to St. Augustine is with a stop at the **Museum Theater**. *Dream of Empire, a Struggle to Survive* is a film describing how Pedro Menéndez de Aviles founded the city and explains how early Spanish settlers lived.

Location:	5 Cordova Street
Hours:	Daily 9–5, closed Christmas
Fees:	Adults $3, children 2–15 $1
Phone:	(904) 824–0339.

Spanish colonial life of the 1740s is recreated in **The Restored Spanish Quarter**. The 19th Century House highlights Florida's Territorial period.

Location:	Entrances at Triay House, St. George St. and opposite Castillo de San Marcos
Hours:	Daily 9–5, closed Christmas
Fees:	Adults $5, seniors (over 62) $4.50, children 6–18 $2, or a family admission $10
Phone:	(904) 825–6830

Many Old City buildings are well worth seeing. The **Oldest House** records life from the early 1700s, through British occupation, and to Flagler's railroading era in the 1890s.

Location:	14 St. Francis Street
Hours:	Daily 9–5, closed Christmas
Fees:	Adults $5, seniors (over 55) $4.50, students $2.50
Phone:	(904) 824–2872

*A walk along the waterfront in
Victorian St. Augustine.*

Henry Morrison Flagler was a major figure in Florida's 20th century economic expansion. Before coming to Florida to retire, he had been senior lieutenant to John D. Rockefeller at Standard Oil Company. While vacationing in St. Augustine, he decided to build a railroad and hotels for wealthy Northerners. Whether or not he ever unretired is incidental. Until his death, Mr. Flagler was committed to building a major railroad network between St. Augustine and Key West.

Now, back to St. Augustine. Imagine being surrounded by the contents of an early *Sears Catalog*. That feeling is reproduced at the *Oldest Store Museum*. Many items date from the 1850s when the store supplied most of the building materials for Mr. Flagler's hotels, church, and railroad. The museum shows over 100,000 items. A good game for children is to ask them to find items they have never seen before, imagine how they would be used today, and then learn how they were used by our ancestors.

Location:	4 Artillery Lane
Hours:	Monday through Saturday 9–5, Sunday noon–5, closed Christmas
Fees:	Adults $3, children 6–12 $1.50
Phone:	(904) 829–9729

Another interesting stop, particularly with children, is *The Oldest Wooden Schoolhouse.* Built of red cedar and cypress, it was put together with wooden pegs and handmade nails. Most kids enjoy seeing books used in schools before the Revolutionary War. They also learn that the schoolmaster and his family were never far away. In fact, they lived above the school.

The Oldest Wooden Schoolhouse

Location:	14 St. George Street
Hours:	Daily 9–5, closed Christmas
Fees:	Adults $1.50, children 6–12 75¢
Phone:	(904) 824–0192

Step inside the *Spanish Military Hospital* to see a ward, an office, and an apothecary dating from 1791.

Location:	Aviles Street
Hours:	Daily 9–5, closed Christmas
Fees:	No charge
Phone:	(904) 825–6830

Ponce de León had been the Spanish Governor of Puerto Rico. Always the explorer, he came to St. Augustine to find new land and to establish a new colony. While exploring in Florida, he was supposed to have heard an old Indian legend about a spring whose water granted eternal youth. Although it is disappointing to accept, it must be emphasized that no literature suggests that he seriously looked for a fountain of youth—and, even worse, there is no evidence that he found one! Facts aside, step right up to the St. Augustine Aquifer at the *The Fountain of Youth* and you, too, can hope for a miracle.

On a more serious note, there is an excellent planetarium at the facility which shows ancient mysteries of navigation and the night skies as they would have appeared during the beginnings of the St. Augustine colony. There is also a brief film that tells of Spanish exploits along the coast, life–sized dioramas of Indian town life, and Ponce de León's landing.

Location:	155 Magnolia Avenue
Hours:	Daily 9–5, closed Christmas
Fees:	Adults $4, seniors (over 55) $4.50, children 6–12 $1.50
Phone:	(904) 829–3168

America's first mission, *Nombre de Dios*, was built in 1565. It commemorates the spot where Pedro Menéndez de Aviles, the founder of St. Augustine, celebrated North America's first mass. An important religious site, it reflects the beginning of the permanent history of Christianity in what is now the United States. A 250–foot tall cross marks the spot where the first cross was planted.

Location:	27 Ocean Avenue
Hours:	Daily 9–6
Fees:	No charge, donations welcome
Phone:	(904) 824–2809

Otto C. Lightner, the founding editor of *Hobbies Magazine,* wintered in St. Augustine. He collected relics of America's Gilded Age including Victorian stained glass items, displayed in a stained glass room created by Louis Comfort Tiffany. The room is part of the *Lightner Museum,* located in what was once Mr. Flagler's *Alcazar Hotel.* Built in 1888, the hotel had the largest enclosed swimming pool in the world. The complex now contains the museum, city offices, an antique mall, and a locally owned, moderately priced restaurant.

Location:	City Hall Complex at King and Cordova Streets
Hours:	Daily 9–5, closed Christmas
Fees:	Adults $4, children 12–18 $1
Phone:	(904) 824–2874

Mr. Flager built the *Memorial Presbyterian Church* in 1890 as a memorial to his daughter who died giving birth to his granddaughter. The baby passed away 10 days later. Step inside this beautiful Venetian Renaissance building for a quiet moment of reflection and to look at the stained glass windows he selected to grace their memories.

Location:	Valencia and Sevilla Streets
Hours:	Monday through Saturday 9–4:30
Fees:	No charge
Phone:	(904) 829–6451

Like the Oldest Schoolhouse, the *Old St. Johns County Jail* served two functions. Built in 1890, it was in continuous service as a jail until 1953 and provided living quarters for the sheriff and his family. Besides viewing the building and learning how criminals were incarcerated in the late 1800s, make time to see the interesting collection of guns and other weaponry. The building is on the National Registry of Historic Sites.

Location:	167 San Marco Avenue
Hours:	Daily 8:30–5, closed Easter, Christmas Eve, and Christmas. The facility is closed through February 1992 for renovation
Fees:	Adults $3.25, children 6–12 $2.25
Phone:	(904) 829–3800

Anastasia Island–St. Augustine Beach

Lighthouses were important along this section of the coast, particularly because of the treacherous currents and coral reefs. Constructed between 1871 and 1874, the *Lighthouse Museum* is housed in the restored Keeper's House and shows how lighthouse keepers and their families lived during that period.

Location:	A1A South, turn left on Old Beach Road
Hours:	Daily 10–5, closed Easter, Thanksgiving, and Christmas
Fees:	**Museum and Lighthouse Tower:** Adults $3.50 **Museum only:** adults $2
Phone:	(904) 829–0745

When the Spanish settled St. Augustine, they crossed the Matanza River to Anastasia Island where they quarried a local building rock called coquina. The quarry is part of the *Anastasia State Recreation Area*. During the 16th and 17th centuries, coquina was one of the most important building materials used in Northeastern Florida. Not particularly attractive, its pitted, oyster shell appearance belies extraordinary strength.

Location:	13406 A1A South at Route 3
Hours:	Daily, 8–sunset
Fees:	$3.25 per car, maximum of 8 people per car
Phone:	(904) 461–2033

If you're in the recreation area between mid–June and late August, be sure to see Florida's State Play, *Cross and Sword*. This performance is staged in an outdoor amphitheater and has a cast of over 50 actors, musicians, and dancers. During the two–hour performance, the audience travels to Spain, the world of King Philip II, and the founding of what is now the United States. Join Captain Pedro Menéndez de Aviles and his Spanish crew as they set foot on these shores on September 8, 1565, learn about the world they discovered, and the world they created.

Location:	1340 A1A South, on the grounds of the Anastasia State Recreation Area
Hours:	Monday through Saturday evenings at 8:30 from **mid–June through late August**
Fees:	Adults $8, seniors (over 65) $7, students (if over 16, ID is required) $4
Phone:	(904) 471–1965

Mandarin

Harriet Beecher Stowe and her family wintered in Mandarin for many years, beginning in the 1880s. Although best known as the author of **Uncle Tom's Cabin,** she wrote **Palmetto Leaves** in her Mandarin home at 12447 Mandarin Road. The book describes the Reconstruction Period after the Civil War.

East Central Florida

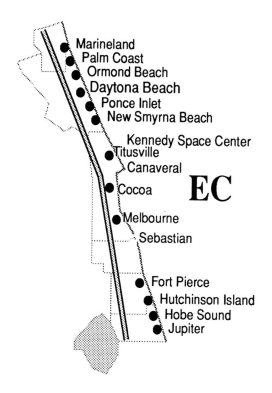

Marineland
Palm Coast
Ormond Beach
Daytona Beach
Ponce Inlet
New Smyrna Beach
Kennedy Space Center
Titusville
Canaveral
Cocoa
EC
Melbourne
Sebastian
Fort Pierce
Hutchinson Island
Hobe Sound
Jupiter

Travelling along A1A down the East Coast of Florida continues the study in contrasts discussed in the earlier tours.

Millionaires, Sand, and Auto Speed Records provides a look backward. Millionaires were among the first people to own automobiles. They spent their holidays refining cars and breaking speed records. This was first done on the sands at Ormond Beach. Tour 3 recognizes one of Florida's particularly illustrious winter citizens. We pause to remember just plain "Neighbor John," known to millions as John D. Rockefeller.

Most first-time visitors to East Central Florida head to *The Space Coast,* described in Tour 4. The *Astronauts Memorial*, rockets, movies, and a bus trip to the launching pad provide days of interesting touring.

Many long-time winter residents travel to Hutchinson Island, Hobe Sound, and Jupiter Inlet. The history of these areas began along *Lighthouse Row.*

Since the 16th century, many ships have been lost off these shores. If you're adventuresome, go to the library to learn about the ship wrecks, and then go scuba diving. Even if you don't find a treasure, being in the water and exploring a 17th century wreck certainly counts as a treasure of a day!

Barney Oldfield in the Blitzen Benz, Daytona Beach, 1910. The Blitzen Benz was built in France specifically to challenge the Stanley Steamer. On March 16, 1910, Barney Oldfield flew through the measured mile time traps to set a new world record of 131.72 miles per hour.

Antique auto buffs gather on Ormond Beach each year to commemorate the Golden Age of auto racing.

Marineland
Palm Coast
Ormond Beach

Tour 3.
Millionaires, Sand, and
Auto Speed Records

Marineland

The original marine life attraction in Florida is *Marineland of Florida*. When the tanks were stocked in May 1938, experts had no experience understanding which species could live together. After some trial and error, the surviving fish began to thrive in the first oceanarium. Features now include continuous dolphin shows, a 3-D movie, and the oceanarium. Although there are many locations in contemporary Florida to watch marine life, this facility is an important example of how the technology began.

Location:	9507 Oceanshore Blvd. (A1A)
Hours:	Labor Day through June 9-5:45; June through Labor Day 9-6
Fees:	Adults $12, seniors (over 65) $10.80, children 3-11 $7
Phone:	(800) 824-4218 (FL), (800) 874-0492 (U.S.)

Palm Coast

Over 390 acres along the Atlantic Ocean and the Matanzas River have been preserved at the *Washington Oaks State Gardens.* Begin your visit on the ocean side. Waves wash away sand exposing a stratum of coquina rock along the picturesque, boulder-strewn beach. Try to plan your visit at low tide to watch many species of shorebirds find dinner around the rocks.

Although the beach area is interesting, my favorite part of the park is across A1A. Once part of the *Belle Vista Plantation* which dates back to 1844, the gardens are located along the Matanzas River. In 1936, Mr. and Mrs. Owen D. Young purchased the property. They were committed to making the site beautiful— they succeeded. After Mr. Young's death, Mrs. Young offered the property to the residents of Florida.

Park guides offer garden tours and there is an interesting interpretive center. This is a good spot for a picnic to enjoy the peace of the riverfront setting, the variety of the ever changing gardens, or the vibrancy of the beachside setting.

Location:	6400 North Oceanshore Boulevard (A1A)
Hours:	Daily 8-sunset. **Tours:** Saturday and Sunday at 1:30
Fees:	$3.25 for car, maximum of 8 people per car
Phone:	(904) 445-3161

Ormond Beach

In 1875, the Corbin Lock Company of New Britain, Connecticut established Ormond as a health center for employees threatened with tuberculosis.

By the latter part of the 19th century, the area became a millionaires' playground. The toys for this beachfront sandbox included the emerging gasoline–powered automobiles. The millionaires brought their cars, their cars' designers, and their stop watches. Speed tests were held regularly on the firmly packed sand.

Ormond claims to be the birthplace of speed. In 1906, a Stanley Steamer driven by Fred Marriott was clocked at 127.66 miles per hour. In 1935, the *Bluebird* reached 276 miles per hour, with Sir Malcolm Campbell driving. Reminders of that early history can be seen in the *Birthplace of Speed Museum*.

Location:	160 Granada Avenue
Hours:	Tuesday through Saturday 10-5
Fees:	$1 per person
Phone:	(904) 672-5657

John D. Rockefeller founded Standard Oil Co. *Henry M. Flagler* was one of his senior lieutenants. They each retired to Florida. Mr. Flagler built the East Coast Railroad and bought or built magnificent hotels, including the Hotel Ormond. Opposite the hotel's golf course, the city's most famous citizen, John D. Rockefeller, purchased *Casements*, a small and unpretentious house.

In other parts of the world, Mr. Rockefeller was known as a ruthless, vigorous, relentless businessman. Particularly as he grew older, the greatest of the trust builders was recognized by townspeople simply as quiet Neighbor John.

Mr. Rockefeller spent his winters at *Casements* from 1914 until his death in 1937. The home has been restored and contains a small museum and a community center. In addition to information about Mr. Rockefeller, this unusual museum contains one of the largest Boy Scout exhibits in the country. There is also a beautiful collection of Hungarian traditional costumes reflecting the area's large Hungarian population.

Location:	25 Riverside Drive
Hours:	Monday through Thursday 9-9, Friday 9-6, Saturday 9-noon, closed holidays
Tours:	Monday through Friday 10 and 2:30, Saturday 10 and 11:30
Fees:	No charge
Phone:	(904) 673-4701

Note *River Bridge*—once the *Ormond Union Church.* Following services, Mr. Rockefeller often stood on the lawn and distributed bright, shiny, new dimes to eager neighborhood children. With the dimes, the children received a mini-sermon outlining the importance of thrift and savings if they wanted to amass a fortune. Although the building is not open to the public, the gardens are a good place to pause for a few moments.

Location:	Opposite Casements

Mr. Rockefeller lived until he was almost 98 years old. He continued to play golf on the Ormond Course until he was almost 90. In his later years, he was usually accompanied on his golf outings by a servant with an umbrella. The servant was responsible for protecting him from the sun. When younger, Mr. Rockefeller had bicycled from stroke to stroke, followed by two valets. One valet was responsible for the milk and crackers; the other carried the golf clubs and a blanket to be spread on the ground when he wished to rest.

He liked to play golf. He loved to win. The story goes that he was once playing with Will Rogers, the noted American humorist. Will Rogers lost the game and said, "I'm glad you beat me, John. The last time you were beaten, I noted that the price of gasoline went up two cents a gallon."

Rockefeller's trouser pockets were always filled with newly minted coins; nickels in one pocket, dimes in the other. Each morning a valet restocked his pockets. The nickels were to encourage the golfer who had played poorly, the dimes were to reward the golfer who beat him. After the 1929 crash, he commented to a partner that he'd have given a nickel for a particular drive, if money weren't so scarce.

As you browse around Ormond Beach, it is fun to think of this amazing American businessman in Ormond's comfortable village setting, the only place in the world where John D. Rockefeller was just Neighbor John.

*John D. Rockefeller attends a fair
sponsored by the Ormond Beach Women's Club, 1926.*

Tour 4.
The Space Frontier

Speed and distance records are destined to be broken. This stretch of uncommon beachfront has had more than its share of opportunity to do just that! Beginning in the early 20th century, auto and motorcycle records have been made and shattered time and time

Daytona Beach
Ponce Inlet
New Smyrna Beach
Kennedy Space Center
Titusville
Canaveral
Cocoa
Melbourne
Sebastian

again. As America's space program developed, this area grew to be one of the major sites from which rockets and shuttles were launched. Tours, exhibits, movies, museums, and an exquisite and moving *Astronaut Memorial* help us appreciate the impact and importance of space exploration.

Daytona Beach

Daytona has been known for setting auto racing records since the turn of the century. During the first decade of the 20th century, the world's speed record of 68 miles per hour, established in 1903 by Andrew Winton, was broken a number of times. In 1910, a new measured mile world record was set on the Daytona Beach sands at 131.92 miles per hour by Barney Oldfield (see photo on page 32). The early races, held on hardpacked sand along the beach, attracted a world class group of serious speedsters and their automobiles.

The beach has been reclaimed by swimmers and their cars. This is one of the few places in Florida where, for a small fee, you can take your family, your picnic, your umbrella, your volleyball, your frisbee, and your vehicle to spend a day at the beach. Enjoy yourself and remember to watch your car at high tide!

The hot spot in Florida for hot cars, hot cycles, and hot spectators is the *Daytona International Speedway*. You can take a 20–minute tour of the Speedway when races are not scheduled. If you like crowds, noise, and a colorful experience, don't miss one of the Race Weeks. During those periods, serious contenders work hard on the track to establish new records. Around the track and throughout the area you can listen to the speedsters talk about racing cars, bikes, accessories, and their improvement.

Location:	1801 Speedway Boulevard, one mile East of I–95
Hours:	Daily 9–5
Fees:	Adults $2, children 6–12 $1
Phone:	To arrange tours: (904) 254–2700, ext. 782
	For tickets: (904) 253–RACE

As you begin a trip down the Space Coast, stop at *Embry– Riddle University*. It is fitting that the only school in the world solely devoted to the study of aviation should be located along the Space Coast. Phone ahead for reservations for an interesting campus tour. Depending upon class schedules, you may be able to see the flight line operations, a wind tunnel, and flight simulators.

Location:	600 South Clyde Morris Boulevard
Hours:	Daily 9–5
Fees:	No charge
Phone:	(904) 226–6000

Throughout Tour 4, the conquering of new frontiers will be described. One of the most important frontiers has been in the area of providing quality education for African American students. *Dr. Mary McLeod Bethune* spent her life working in this area. The Foundation named in her honor is on the *Bethune–Cookman College* campus.

Dr. Bethune, daughter of a freed slave, had a vision of an academy for black students. She knew what the school could be and was single–minded in sharing that vision with others. Although she had no money, she helped a generation of supporters, benefactors, students, and statesmen understand her idea and help her expand it. Her one–room academy opened in 1904 and has grown into the college you see here today.

Although Dr. Bethune's work led her to focus on national education issues, the College remains an important reminder of the her work.

Location:	640 2nd Avenue
Hours:	Monday through Friday 9–5 during the school term
Fees:	No charge
Phone:	(904) 255–1401

The next stop is fun for young kids as well as their parents and grandparents. Although most of this trip is focused on outer space, the *Museum of Arts and Sciences* also reminds us of Florida's inner space. Kids enjoy looking at the skeleton of a giant ground sloth, estimated to be 130,000 years old. Its remains were found near the museum grounds and visually show another Florida tourist or resident from earlier times.

Located on the 60– acre Tuscawilla Park Reserve, the museum also has an extensive Cuban collection of fine and folk art, an American Wing with materials dating to the 1640s, and a planetarium.

Skeleton of the Giant Ground Sloth

Location:	1040 Museum Boulevard
Hours:	**Museum:** Tuesday through Friday 9–4, Saturday and Sunday 12–5, closed major holidays. **Planetarium shows:** Tuesday through Sunday at 1 and 3
Fees:	**Museum and Planetarium:** Adults $3, children and students with ID $1. Wednesday and Friday, no charge for museum, $3 charge for planetarium
Phone:	(904) 255–0285

Port Orange

Once a thriving sugar mill and plantation, the *Sugar Mill Gardens* now include 12 acres of botanical gardens. Of particular interest is the pioneer garden and Ivy Lane, containing 47 varieties of ivy thriving in Florida's climate. Only ruins remain of the buildings. However, ruins can be perfect to provide a framework for youngsters to create their own story of how life could have been lived on a thriving plantation.

Location:	Old Sugar Mill Road
Hours:	Daily 8–5
Fees:	No charge
Phone:	(904) 767–1735

Ponce Inlet

Ponce De Leon Inlet Lighthouse

The 175–foot–tall *Ponce de León Inlet Lighthouse* was built in 1884 and has been dark since 1970. It is the second tallest lighthouse in the country. Climb the 203 steps to the topmost area open to visitors and enjoy a spectacular panoramic view of the inlet, the land, and the sea. There is a 15–minute video on the history of the area and five buildings to explore, including the lighthouse keeper's homes.

Location:	4931 South Peninsula Drive
Hours:	Winter 10–4, Summer 10–8
Fees:	Adults $3, children 2–11 $1
Phone:	(904) 761–1821

New Smyrna Beach

An early Indian village named Caparaca was once located in this area. It is believed that Ponce de León landed near the village in 1513. The first large, well–recorded European settlement in the area occurred about 250 years later when a group of over 1,000 Scottish, Greek, and Italian settlers arrived in 1767. They stayed for nine years and moved on after years of dealing with hurricanes, Indian attacks, and what was to them an unfamiliar and inhospitable natural environment.

You may want to pick up a copy of *The Open Boat*, by Stephen Crane. This makes particularly good beachside reading in this area since Mr. Crane was shipwrecked just off the coast in 1897. He was rescued in a small lifeboat which drifted toward Daytona Beach. The wooden boat broke apart near shore. Fortunately, he was rescued once again. His gripping narrative gives one increased respect for the weather, the shoals, and the hazards of ocean travel in those days. It also serves as a quiet reminder of the role played by the lighthouse keepers and the men we will meet in the next tour who staffed the Houses of Refuge along the shore.

Mr. Crane's experience notwithstanding, New Smyrna Beach is one of the safest spots to swim along this coast. There is a protective rock ledge well offshore that reduces the force of the undercurrents reaching the beach. So, if you're in the mood for an ocean swim, and are travelling with younger children, pause here.

Lazy Afternoon on the Beach

Titusville

Titusville is our starting point for the true Space Coast portion of this trip. The Mercury astronauts are featured within the *United States Astronaut Hall of Fame*. Videotapes of Mercury flight segments are shown. They help bring the era to life as do the personal mementos and equipment donated by the astronauts.

Location:	6225 Vectorspace Boulevard
Hours:	Daily 9–6
Fees:	Adults $4.95, 10% discount for seniors, children under 12 $2.95
Phone:	(407) 268–4716

At some point during their growing up years, many children dream of life on other planets and travelling into space. The *U.S. Space Camp* provides an opportunity for fourth through seventh graders to almost experience space. This five–day summer program teaches the history of the American space program through hands–on experiences—including a simulated space shuttle mission.

Some adults have never completely stopped wishing they could travel into space. The Space Coast Tour provides a way for you to almost do so! Choose a favorite youngster and become part of the Parent–Child Weekend Camp. When you check in you receive a space log, live "on board," eat astronaut food, build a launch rocket, and experience a space simulation—and do it all in a weekend. If interested, book your space adventure well in advance.

Location:	6225 Vectorspace Boulevard
Hours and Fees:	**Space camp**: Fees per participant. Summer $550; Spring and Fall $450 **Parent/Child Weekend**: Per parent/child team $400
Phone:	(407) 267–3184; (407) 269–6100

Merritt Island

The tour now moves from outer space to surface space as we explore the next frontier. The mission of the **Merritt Island National Wildlife Refuge** is to preserve endangered species. The site and staff do it very well as this 140,000–acre refuge is home to more endangered species than any other area of the continental U.S. Although the viewing is always impressive, many people suggest that the very best time for a first visit is between December and March when wood storks, roseate spoonbills, scrub jays, and red shouldered hawks can be observed. Don't forget to look up to watch for the Southern bald eagles that often soar overhead.

Location:	Highway 402, 4 miles east of Titusville
Hours:	Daily 8–4:30
Fees:	No charge
Phone:	(407) 867–0667

John F. Kennedy Space Center

NASA's Spaceport USA needs little introduction. Most Americans have grown up watching launches and learning about space exploration. It is recommended that you spend at least a day here. There is so much to do and see that the following is offered to briefly highlight some of what you may choose to do.

Consider beginning your visit at the **Astronaut Memorial** to pay homage to the U.S. Astronauts who gave their lives to further space exploration.

Since they are often booked hours in advance, plan an early stop to purchase tickets and reserve your space for one or both of the **Bus Tours**.

On the *Red Tour,* you experience a simulated launch from the site where all the Apollo astronauts trained, inspect a Saturn V rocket (it's longer than a football field), and see the massive six million pound crawler transporters that carry space shuttles to their launch pads. It's also possible to take a close look at the two pads where all the space shuttles lift off.

...and launch!

On the *Blue Tour,* visit the Cape Canaveral Air Force Station where the history of the early space program unfolds. There is also a stop at the *Air Force Space Museum* and the opportunity to see the sites where the first astronauts were launched in the Mercury and Gemini programs.

Two fine films are shown. *The Boy from Mars* screens continuously in the Galaxy Theater. *The Dream is Alive* is an I–MAX film showing footage of early earth shots by astronauts who were space travellers on several shuttle missions.

The museums have such rich collections it would be easy to spend a day visiting them only. Try to make time to see *The Gallery of Spaceflight Museum.* It includes such items as a Gemini space suit, a full–size model of a Lunar Rover, and a moon rock. *The NASA Art Gallery* shows more than 250 paintings and sculptures created by artists commissioned by the NASA Art Program and the *Rocket Garden* is an impressive way to realize the advances made in rocketry. *Satellites and You* is a 45–minute exhibit that uses robotic astronauts to demonstrate how satellites affect life on earth.

Location:	Kennedy Space Center, Route 405
Hours:	Daily 9–7:30, closed Christmas
Fees:	**Bus Tour:** Adults $6, children $3. **I–MAX Film:** Adults $2.75, children $1.75
Phone:	(407) 452–2121

44

Canaveral

One of the last truly undeveloped beaches on the East Coast is part of the *Canaveral National Seashore*. The area is a sanctuary for at least 15 endangered species as well as winter quarters for thousands of migratory birds. It is primitive and parking is at a premium. Should you go? Absolutely—and only when you have time to stop wearing a watch and start watching the environment. Earlier cultures lived in this area and there are still at least 60 undeveloped sites dating from the Indian and Spanish settlement periods. So, go exploring. Who knows what you'll see.

Location:	Directly north of the Kennedy Space Center
	Follow A1A until it dead ends off Route 44
Hours:	Daily 6 am–sunset, visitor center daily 7:30–4:30,
	Playalinda Beach closed on days when there is a
	shuttle on the launch pad
Fees:	No charge
Phone:	(407) 267–1110

Cocoa

Who would name a town after a breakfast drink? There's an interesting and supposedly true story to be told. Originally called Indian River City, the U.S. Post Office told the townspeople their community's name was too long. They had to change it. What a problem! Everyone had a favorite name. Finally, a meeting was held in the general store. Names were presented and rejected all evening. No consensus was reached. As the meeting was about to break up, someone noticed a tin of cocoa on the store's shelf. As a joke, the suggestion was made that the town be named Cocoa. They liked it, and voted it in, and—we presume—went home for a commemorative cup of cocoa.

A few groups have been having telescope problems recently. The *Astronaut Memorial Space Science Center and Planetarium* is no exception. However, as soon as it's repaired, this is the place to come to look through the state's largest public telescope. In the meantime, there are several other telescopes available for viewing, as well as a model of John Glenn's space capsule, and an excellent planetarium show.

Location:	1519 Clearlake Road, Brevard Commmunity College
Hours:	**Exhibits**: Monday through Friday 9–5. **Observatory** (weather permitting): Friday and Saturday nights to 10 pm. **Planetarium**: Wednesday and Friday at 4, Friday at 7 and 8. **Laser shows:** Friday and Saturday at 9 and 10
Fees:	**Exhibits and Observatory**: No charge. **Planetarium:** Adults $3, seniors and children $2 **Laser show** $4
Phone:	(407) 631–7889

Melbourne

There are several galleries in the state which have been designed for the visually impaired and one of them is at the *Brevard Art Center and Museum.* The museum features 19th and 20th century animal sculptures, Japanese woodblock prints, and American paintings.

Location:	1463 North Highland Avenue
Hours:	Tuesday through Friday 10– 5; Saturday 10–4, Sunday 12–4
Fees:	Adults $2
Phone:	(407) 242–0737

Give the kids a chance to launch the Earth into orbit, test their shark IQ, or find buried treasure at the *Space Coast Science Center.*

Location:	1510 Highland Avenue
Hours:	Tuesday through Saturday 10–5, Sunday 12–5
Fees:	Adults $3, seniors (over 60) $2, children 3–17 $1.50
Phone:	(407) 259–5572

One of the few large–scale reminders of the cattle frontier that can still be seen in Florida is the *Deseret Ranch.* Purchased during the 1950s by the Mormon Church, it is the second largest cow–calf operation in the U.S. The cattle, citrus, and timber ranch covers approximately 300,000 acres between Melbourne and St. Cloud. Although most of the property is used for agriculture and farming, from time to time there are suggestions that a new community may be developed on a small portion of the land in the future.

Call ahead if you'd like to arrange a one hour driving tour conducted by a retired cowhand who tells old cowboy stories along the way.

Location:	Route 419 off Route 192 between Melbourne and St. Cloud
Hours:	Tours by appointment only
Fees:	No charge
Phone:	(407) 892–3672

Melbourne Beach

The eleven–mile strip of coast between Melbourne Beach and Sebastian Inlet is the nation's largest nesting area for endangered *loggerhead sea turtles*. From late May through September, it is possible to spend an evening watching sea turtles lumber ashore to deposit eggs in the sand. Sea turtle watches are planned by the Audubon Society and nature and science centers along this part of the coastline as well as on Merritt Island, Hutchinson Island, Jensen Beach, and Sebastian Inlet. Try to make arrangements to spend an evening with the sea, the moon, the turtles, and a park naturalist—you won't forget the experience.

Sebastian Inlet

In July of 1715, eleven fully loaded Spanish treasure ships left Cuba to return to Spain. They were blown off course by a terrible hurricane and all the boats were wrecked off the Sebastian shore. A *Survivor's Camp* was set up on the site of what is now the *McLarty State Museum*. Runners went up and down the beach to find the waterlogged sailors. In this way, 1,500 people were saved.

From 1715 through 1719, the survivors worked at salvage operations to regain the sunken treasure. Many valuable items were found and shipped back to Spain. Many of the treasures have still not surfaced. Within the museum there is an excellent 15–minute slide show telling this story as well as dioramas showing how the survivors lived.

Divers search for treasure in the area between Sebastian Inlet and St. Lucie's Inlet. They look in the area 300–400 yards off the coast in 20 feet of water. Don't be surprised the first time you see scuba–geared treasure hunters carrying their metal detectors into the sea. They use these 20th century sounding devices to help them find coins and other treasures in the turbulent water.

Location:	5–1/4 miles North of Route 510 on A1A at the South end of the Sebastian Inlet State Recreation Area
Hours:	Daily 10–4
Fees:	General admission $1
Phone:	(407) 589–2147

As a brief footnote on history, the Ringling brothers made the tiny fishing village of Sebastian Inlet their first Florida circus home. During the summer months, they toured the Midwestern countryside as musicians and billed their act as the *Ringling Brothers' Moral, Elevating, Instructive and Fascinating Concert and Variety Performance.* That was certainly a lot harder to say than their later slogan, *The Greatest Show on Earth.* As their show grew, winter headquarters moved to Florida's West Coast.

Pelican Island, the nation's oldest wildlife sanctuary, was established on the island in 1903 by President Theodore Roosevelt. No visitors are permitted, so please anchor near the shore to observe the birds and animals. If you have questions, phone the Merritt Island National Wildlife Refuge at (407) 876–0667.

Pelican in Profile

Tour 5.
Lighthouse
Row

As you may have noticed, the character of the Atlantic coastline changes from tour to tour and the area covered along Lighthouse Row tour is no exception. For people who enjoy quiet elegance and beautiful natural scenery, this stretch of beach may become an all–time favorite.

Hutchinson Island

Several American inventors came to Florida at the turn of the century. One who lived and worked in the area was Sterling Elliott. The **Eliott Museum** features reproductions of fourteen early shops and inventions covering the period from 1865–1930.

Location:	825 Northeast Ocean Boulevard
Hours:	Daily
Fees:	Adults $2.50, children 6–13 50¢
Phone:	(407) 225–1961

A natural next stop involves inventions of another kind. During World War II, underwater demolition teams of the U.S. Navy trained in the area. Their contribution to the war effort is highlighted at the **Underwater Demolition Team–SEAL Museum**. We particularly enjoyed seeing the former top secret midget submarines which are on display. Be sure to see the video presentation highlighting the training processes used and the exhibits tracing the exploits of Navy divers from 1944 to astronaut landings at sea.

Location:	3300 North A1A, North Hutchinson Island
Hours:	Tuesday through Saturday 10–4, Sunday 12–4
Fees:	Adults $1, children 6–11, 50¢
Phone:	(407) 489–3597

One of the most important locations along this coast at the turn of the century was the *Gilbert's Bar House of Refuge*. In the old days, ship captains had to rely on maps and visual sightings to avoid the treacherous hidden reefs along the Atlantic Coast as well as the fierce storms common during some seasons of the year. In the late 1800s, 10 refuge stations were built along the Eastern coast and the one you will see was built in 1875.

The refuge keeper's mission was to find and save shipwrecked sailors and their passengers. To do this, he would walk the beach each morning and after storms, looking for survivors. When he found them, he would take them back to the House of Refuge and care for them until they were well. The boathouse displays articles from shipwrecks, with items in the permanent collection dating back to the 1700s.

Location:	301 Southeast MacArthur Boulevard
Hours:	Tuesday through Sunday 1–4:15, closed holidays
Fees:	Adults $1 children 6–13 50¢
Phone:	(407) 225–1875

Hobe Sound

The drive between Hobe Sound and Jupiter is particularly beautiful. Many winter visitors decided against the visible wealth of the Palm Beach area and formed a quiet, exclusive enclave along the Hobe Sound beachfront. Be prepared for waterfront estates and subdued elegance. There is a public beach at the Hobe Sound end of the drive.

One of Florida's earliest surviving journals was written by Jonathan Dickinson. A Quaker, he and his family were shipwrecked off this coast in the 1690s. They were rescued by Indians on Hobe Sound. After many adventures, they arrived safely in St. Augustine. Mr. Dickinson kept a detailed journal entitled *God's Protecting Providence*. Look for it in your library. It is a fascinating story of the lives and activities of the Florida Indians and their interactions with the early settlers.

The highlight of the *Jonathan Dickinson State Park* is the *Foxahatchee River*, which is the only National Wild and

Scenic River in Florida (over 90 per cent of these rivers are in the Western portions of the country). There are hiking trails and canoe rentals near the river. Consider a 1–1/2–hour canoe trip to the **Trapper Nelson Interpretive Center** where a 30–minute Park Ranger program is highly recommended.

Location:	16450 Southeast Federal Highway
Hours:	Daily 8–sunset
Fees:	$3.25 per car, maximum of 8 people per vehicle
Phone:	(407) 546–2771

Canoe journey observed

Tequesta

Archaeological evidence shows that Indian tribes lived here more than 2,500 years ago. One of the natural wonders at the site is the largest outcropping of Anastasia limestone on the Atlantic Coast. **Blowing Rocks Preserve** is well named. At high tide whale spouts of water push through the limestone rock and create everchanging natural fountain displays. There is very little parking available, so plan to go early.

Location:	A1A about 3 miles North of Jupiter Inlet
Hours:	Daily 9–5, limited parking
Fees:	No charge

51

Jupiter

Part of the early history of the Southeastern coast of Florida involved the legendary *Barefoot Mailman*. In the old days, before roads or tourists or railroads or superhighways, it was a challenge to get mail between Jupiter and Miami. The safest and fastest way was, literally, to walk the mail through. The mailman walked along the beach and swam or rowed across the inlets. This was one of the more dedicated ways in which the U.S. Post Office maintained its delivery schedule!

Although the importance of lighthouses has diminished during the past quarter century, they remain an important part of the culture of the Florida coast. You may want to enjoy a late afternoon pause, stop at one of several waterfront restaurants, and enjoy looking at the *Jupiter Inlet Lighthouse*.

The Jupiter Inlet Lighthouse

Southeastern Florida

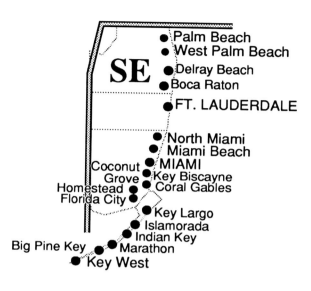

We see more contrasts as the trip down Florida's East Coast continues. The next several tours travel from the opulence of Palm Beach to the bustle of Miami, which is one of Florida's international cities. You then go to the deserted wilderness of the Everglades, and finally to Key West at the Southernmost tip of the state, a longtime haven of artists and authors.

Tour 6 notes American opulence. Florida's *Gold Coast* includes the Palm Beach area where mansions line the tour route.

Miami has a rich, varied history. Within Tour 7, *The Miami Seven*—the city's "neighborhoods"—are isolated to show a glimpse of the internationalism and variety of this cosmopolitan city.

Tour 8, *The River of Grass*, leads you into an ecologically critical area, larger than the state of Rhode Island. The Everglades have a rhythm of their own and provide a noted contrast to Miami's urban vibrancy.

Hemingway's Haunts come to life as you drive Tour 9 along the magnificent, waterbound Florida Keys. The tour ends in Key West, a city unlike any other in Florida.

Henry Morrison Flagler, Engraving by J. J. Cade

●Palm Beach
● West Palm Beach
●Delray Beach
●Boca Raton
●FT. LAUDERDALE

Tour 6.
The
Gold
Coast

Palm Beach

In 1878 a Spanish barque was wrecked off the shore of what is now Palm Beach. The vessel carried a cargo of coconuts. They were washed ashore and took root. In time the barren sand key was transformed into a beautiful tropical island.

Henry Morrison Flager saw the island and its possibilities in 1893. During this period he was expanding his railroad empire down the coast of Florida and identifying sites for future luxury hotels. He directed the layout of Palm Beach township, built the Royal Poinciana Hotel, and established Palm Beach as a winter retreat for the very, very wealthy.

For many years no wheeled vehicles, with the exception of bicycles and two–passenger bicycled rickshaw–like vehicles, were allowed on the island. Today, from December to March, the town's resident multimillionaires and their vintage cars are visible along **Worth Avenue**, the community's primary shopping street.

One example of the opulence of the Palm Beach Golden Era open to the public is the **Henry M. Flagler Museum.** His collection is housed in **Whitehall**, a magnificent mansion which was Mr. Flagler's wedding gift to his third wife, Mary Lily Kenan. It was built in 1901 at a cost of $2.5 million with an additional $1.5 million spent on furnishings.

The architecture shows a strong Spanish influence with the rooms built around a central courtyard. As one of Florida's major railroad entrepreneurs, it is fitting that Henry Flagler's private railroad car is also available for viewing.

Location: Cocoanut Row at Whitehall Way
Hours: Tuesday through Saturday 10–5, Sunday 12–5.
              Closed Christmas and New Year
Fees: Adults $5, children $2
Phone: (407) 655–2833

Whitehall, the Flagler's Palm Beach Home

Although Mr. Flagler created Palm Beach, Addison Mizner, architect, prize fighter, and miner, placed his signature upon the town. Many of the Palm Beach Mediterranean–style mansions built during the 1920s were his work. He introduced the Spanish vogue that resulted in a transformation of architecture all along Florida's lower East Coast. His houses were built with courtyards on various levels and had exposed rafters and vaulted ceilings. To obtain the materials needed for these creations, Mr. Mizner established his own factories to manufacture tile, ironwork, furniture, and pottery. He created some of the most beautiful homes in Palm Beach and moved on to Boca Raton.

It would have been fun to see all the architects who were working in Palm Beach in the 1920s. *The Breakers*, a landmark hotel of Italian Renaissance design, was built in 1925. It was designed by the New York architectural firm of Schulze and Weaver (that firm also designed the Waldorf–Astoria). One of our favorite ways to explore The Breakers is after enjoying the bountiful Sunday Brunch.

Location:	One South County Road
Phone:	(407) 654–8403

It is an easy walk from The Breakers to *Bethesda–by–the–Sea.* A Gothic–style Episcopal church, its architecture is reminiscent of 15th century English churches. Stop to see the building and then pause to walk slowly through the adjacent *Cluett Memorial Garden.*

Location:	144 South County Road (Northeast Corner at Barton Avenue)
Hours:	Daily 8–4
Fees:	No charge
Phone:	(407) 655–4554

A pleasant, longer walk is to follow the route of *The Bicycle Trail.* It covers 4.8 miles of magnificent scenery and architecture and is probably the best way to explore the area.

Locaton:	Begin the self–guided tour South of the Royal Park Bridge at Four Seasons Plaza

West Palm Beach

West Palm Beach had its first growth surge in the late 1800s. It was almost entirely populated by people working on Mr. Flagler's new Palm Beach hotel, the Royal Poinciana. In those days, there were no bridges connecting Palm Beach to West Palm Beach. At Mr. Flagler's instruction, all the guests, supplies, and day workers were ferried back and forth. Mr. Flagler wanted to exclude all visible business enterprise from Palm Beach. As time passed, bridges connected the two communities. However, in many ways, West Palm Beach continues to serve as the business center for nearby Palm Beach.

The Norton Gallery of Art is one of Florida's major museums. It is distinguished by its outstanding permanent collec–

tions including French Impressionists, 20th century American art, Chinese bronzes, and jade.

Location:	1451 South Olive Avenue
Hours:	Tuesday through Saturday 10–5, Sunday 1–5, closed Mondays and major holidays
Fees:	No charge, donations welcome
Phone:	(407) 832–5194

Delray Beach

Many members of the Yamato Colony of Japanese settlers brought their farming techniques and skills to Delray Beach in the early 1900s. One of the original members of the Colony was George Sukeji Morikami. His major gift permitted the growth of the *Morikami Park, Museum and Japanese Gardens*. The facility honors the memories of the early Japanese settlers. There are nearly 200 acres of nature trails, gardens, a cultural center, and an excellent bonsai exhibit.

This site is so tranquil that we urge you to plan an unstructured, leisurely visit. Of course, if you do this you will have time for tea and a careful look at the museum's treasures. Besides the exhibits, the Morikami presents many events during the year which highlight Japanese culture and festivals. You may wish to phone ahead and ask for a copy of their schedule.

Location:	4000 Morikami Park Road
Hours:	Tuesday through Sunday and holidays 10–5, closed Easter, July 4, Thanksgiving, Christmas, and New Year's Day
Fees:	No charge, donations welcome
Phone:	(407) 495–0233

Boca Raton

Boca Raton is now a lovely resort and business community which has had several lives. In the 18th and 19th centuries it was a terrifying, rough–and–ready pirate's cove.

By the early 1920s, Addison Mizner had traveled down the coast from Palm Beach. He had grand ideas for a luxury resort.

The Mizner Development Corporation bus waits to transport prospective property buyers from Miami to Boca Raton.

Miami, 1925

Mr. Mizner had grand ideas for his property in Boca Raton. He wanted to build a canal and gondola to carry wealthy visitors to his beautiful Spanish–Gothic inn which opened in 1926. Although the canal was never built, the stately boulevard provides a good setting for the main building of the ***Boca Raton Hotel and Club***.

Location:	Camino Real
Phone:	(305) 395–3000

Singing Pines, the second oldest house in Boca Raton was built in 1912 and has been carefully restored to reflect that period. The building now houses ***The Children's Museum***, providing hands–on activities for children from 4–12. Two of the favorite exhibits are the pioneer kitchen and a child–scale working supermarket exhibit.

Location:	498 Crawford Boulevard
Hours:	Tuesday through Saturday, 12–5
Fees:	Children $1
Phone:	(407) 368–6875

In much the same way that earlier millionaires along the East Coast embraced automobiles and auto racing, many of today's millionaires turn to polo, the international sport of kings.

A Polo Match in Progress

There are outstanding *Polo Clubs* in many Southern Florida communities. Phone the Royal Palm Club in Boca Raton or the Palm Beach Polo Club and ask about the schedule. It's fun to enjoy a winter afternoon watching players, polo ponies, and spectators. Games are usually held on Wednesday and Sunday afternoons during the season which extends from January through April.

Fort Lauderdale

Once a hot, steamy mangrove swamp, a U.S. Fort was constructed on the site in 1838 to guard against the Seminole Indians. Named for its commander, Major William Lauderdale, it remained open until 1857. Then all was quiet in the sleepy shorefront hamlet until Henry Flagler's railroad reached the site in 1911. With the arrival of the steam engine, travel to Fort Lauderdale became easy. Many people worked to capitalize on the real estate opportunities.

Charles Rodes is largely responsible for 20th century Fort Lauderdale. He studied the parallel canal system used in Venice and transferred the concept to America. There are now more than

300 miles of navigable inland waterways in the Greater Fort Lauderdale area. Impressive homes, imposing docks, and beautiful yachts line many of the canals. There is a water taxi which travels along the canal and can be boarded from many of the major waterside hotels. After a watery ride, the town's nickname, The Venice of America, seems quite appropriate.

The only home in Florida which is directly administered by the Florida Trust for Historic Preservation is the *Bonnet House*. Mr. Frederic Clay Bartlett was a Chicago art collector and muralist. His first wife, Helen Birch Bartlett, was the daughter of one of Florida's early philanthropists. As a wedding gift, her father gave the couple 36 acres in what is now downtown Fort Lauderdale.

The Bartletts decided to build a home and an environment. Unlike the Spanish and Mediterranean styles then in vogue along the East Coast, the Bartletts chose to build a tropical plantation house. With an open, simple design, it has a two–story veranda and rooms wrapping around a large courtyard. When visiting, look closely at the animal murals and carousel carvings. Evelyn, Mr. Bartlett's second wife was also a painter. Her imagination is clearly evident in the whimsical mood of this important landmark site.

The house serves as a perfect backdrop for the luxurious exotic gardens created. The yellow Bonnet water lilies that grow on two small ponds on the property are particularly lovely, and the house is named for them. Arrange to tour this impressive house, the gardens, and Mr. Bartlett's painting studio.

Location:	900 North Birch Road
Hours:	Guided tours on Tuesday, Thursday, and Saturday at 10 am and 1:30 pm. Phone ahead for reservations
Fees:	Adults and children over 6 $7.50, seniors and military personnel $5
Phone:	(305) 563–5393

Time for another just–for–children stop. *The Discovery Center Museum* is a childrens' hands–on, participatory science, art, and history facility housed in what was once Ft. Lauderdale's first hotel.

Location:	231 Southwest 2nd Avenue
Hours:	Mid–June through August: Tuesday through Saturday 10–5, Sunday 12–5. Rest of year: Tuesday through Saturday 10–5. Closed Thanksgiving, Christmas, and New Year's Day
Fees:	General admission $2
Phone:	(305) 462–6536

If you care about competitive swimming, diving, water polo, synchronized swimming and water safety, the *International Swimming Hall of Fame Aquatic Complex –Museum and Pool* is the place to see. There are movies, medals, trophies, and action exhibits highlighting the accomplishments of more than 300 aquatic greats. Bring a bathing suit. Your style and speed might improve in these championship pools!

Location:	501 Seabreeze Boulevard
Hours:	**Hall of Fame**: Monday through Saturday 10–5, Sunday 11–4. **Pools**: Daily 10–4
Fees:	**Hall of Fame**: Adults $4, seniors (over 65), military personnel and students $2, family rate $10. **Pools**: Adults $3, seniors (over 65), military personnel and students $2, children under 6 $1.50
Phone:	(305) 462–6536

The Tequesta Indians played a major role in this area. The *Museum of Archaeology* houses permanent displays of natural history featuring the Tequesta Indians, geology, African tribal arts, pre–Columbian artifacts, and marine archaeology.

Location:	203 Southwest 1st Avenue
Hours:	Tuesday through Saturday 10–4, Sunday 1–4
Fees:	Adults $1, children 50¢
Phone:	(305) 525–8778

One of the largest collections of ethnographic material in Florida is housed at the *Museum of Art*. The collection includes Oceanic, West African, pre–Columbian, and American Indian works. The museum also shows American and European art.

Location: One East Las Olas Boulevard
Hours: Tuesday 11–9, Wednesday through Saturday
               10–5, Sunday 12–5
Fees: Adults $3.25, seniors (over 65) $2.75, students with
               ID $1
Phone: (305) 525–5500

S tranahan House is the oldest home on its original site in Broward County. It was originally a trading post for Seminole Indians from the Everglades. The building has been restored to show how it looked in the 1913–1915 period, providing an interesting glimpse of how people lived in early Fort Lauderdale.

Location: 335 Southeast 6th Avenue
Hours: September through June: Wednesday, Friday, and
               Saturday 10–3:30. Friday evening socials and tours
               are held from 5:30–8. Closed Thanksgiving,
               Christmas and New Year's Day
Fees: Adults $3, children under 12 $2
Phone: (305) 524–4736

Just a few miles inland in Coconut Creek is ***Butterfly World.*** A screened–in tropical rain forest houses over 150 species of colorful butterflies. Visit for the afternoon when they are most active. We feel this is a must–see stop!

Location: 3600 West Sample Road in Tradewinds Park South
Hours: Monday through Saturday 9–5, Sunday 1–5.
               Closed Thanksgiving and Christmas
Fees: Adults $7.50, Seniors (over 60) $6, children 3–12
               $5
Phone: (305) 977–4400

Explore Miami. It will surprise you! We begin the Miami Seven section of the tour with two images—one dating from 1930, the other relatively recent.

Miami Theater District,
November 18, 1930

Miami Skyline

North Miami
Miami Beach
Coconut Grove MIAMI
Key Biscayne
South Miami Coral Gables

Seven metropolitan Miami communities are highlighted as part of this tour. Each area has a different personality. When you have completed the trip you will have a better understanding of the city's cosmopolitan, international nature.

One cautionary comment should be made. Miami has been a difficult city for tourists in the recent past. Watch your belongings, realize you're in a large, metropolitan, multinational, multicultural city, and act accordingly. Ask for the Chamber of Commerce's recent publication on safety tips for tourists—and follow them!

Miami

Long, long ago a shipwrecked sailor was saved by the Tequesta Indians and lived among them near Lake Okeechobee. The Indians named the place the *Lake of Mayaime.* The name was shortened to Miami, Tequestan for "sweet water."

What changes have happened to the area since that ship-wrecked sailor's experiences! European settlement began, the harbor area became a Spanish stronghold, and an American fort was built to protect the early settlers from the Indians.

By the late 1800s, Miami had become a small, quiet fishing village. Transportation to other parts of Florida was slow and difficult. There were no overland roads and most settlers came by sea. As we noted earlier, even getting mail through from Jupiter was a challenging experience.

Then came a few hearty Northerners seeking the mild winter climate. Miami's 20th century evolution was about to begin.

Julia Tuttle, a displaced Clevelander, understood Miami's potential. She single–handedly became the city's greatest promoter. She met Henry Flagler and later wrote to him in glowing terms about the area's superb winter weather. She urged him to extend his railroad empire all the way to Miami and she convinced him. The rest, as they say, is history.

Julia Tuttle, Miami Pioneer

Mr. Flagler's expansion of the railroad brought other developers and the city became a winter resort. Over the decades, an influx of Latin Americans began. This was partially prompted by political unrest in several Caribbean and South American countries, escalating in the 1960s with the migration of Cubans. Miami is now a melting pot of Caribbean, Central, North, and South American cultures.

An interesting first stop to begin to understand the diversity of the area is *The Historical Museum of South Florida and the Caribbean.*

Location: Miami–Dade Cultural Center, 101 West Flagler
Hours and Fees: Please note information for Center for the Fine Arts
Phone: (305) 375–1492

The Center for the Fine Arts is dedicated solely to the display of large–scale, changing exhibitions.

Location: Miami–Dade Cultural Center, 101 West Flagler
Hours: Tuesday through Saturday 10–5, Thursday 10–9, Sunday noon–5. Closed Thanksgiving, Christmas and New Year's Day
Fees: Adults $5, children 6–12 $3 (this is a combination ticket with the Historical Museum, see above)
Phone: (305) 375–1700

It's hard to think of the opulence of the rich in the early days of the 20th century. Difficult, that is, until one visits *Vizcaya*. James Deering, Vice President of International Harvester, wanted to create a special winter retreat. After much deliberation with architects, art dealers, and art historians, building began in 1916.

Vizcaya grew to become Mr. Deering's personal celebration of the European decorative arts, with the museum representing the Renaissance, Baroque, Rococo, and Neoclassic periods. The villa's 70 rooms are arranged around a central courtyard. Thirty–four rooms are open for public viewing. The guided tours are highly recommended and last for about 45 minutes.

The gardens invite contemplation and reflection. One of the exceptional areas is the *Ellis A. Gimbel Garden for the Blind*, founded in 1984. Close your eyes to fully experience the unique textures, smells, and sounds.

Location:	3251 South Miami Avenue (just South of Rickenbacker Causeway entrance)
Hours:	Daily 9:30–4:30, closed Christmas
Fees:	Adults $8, children 6–18 $4
Phone:	(305) 579–2708

Children can learn about light, sound, electronics, biology, and energy at the *Miami Museum of Science and Space Transit Planetarium*. The *Animal Exploratorium* features live giant insects, reptiles, and marine life. Save time to experience space transit via *The Black Hole,* part of the planetarium's imaginative laser show.

Location:	3280 South Miami Avenue
Hours:	Daily 10–6, closed Thanksgiving and Christmas, observatory open Thursday through Sunday 8–10 pm, weather permitting
Fees:	Adults $6, seniors (over 65) and children 3–12 $4,
Phone:	(305) 854–4247

When you need an oasis in the midst of the busy city, try *Bayfront Park*. It combines monuments and spaces for quiet reflection. Walk through the park and pause to honor such interna–

tional heroes as Christopher Columbus and José Cecello del Valle, who wrote Honduras' federal constitution. Look for the John F. Kennedy Memorial Torch of Friendship symbolizing friendship between Miami and Latin American countries.

Bayside is a nearby area of colorful shops, restaurants, and entertainment on an outdoor stage. This is an interesting spot to pause to enjoy the waterfront.

Location: Foot of Biscayne Boulevard

There is no place like it in the world. Bring an atlas to help you recognize the home ports of the magnificent passenger liners you will see docked at the *Port of Miami*, the largest cruise passenger facility in the world. Watch the efficiency with which the passengers, luggage, and thousands of items that make trips enjoyable are loaded onto the giant liners.

Location: 1/2 mile East of Biscayne Blvd.

For many new Miami residents, the *Freedom Tower* served as the equivalent to earlier generations' Statue of Liberty and Ellis Island. The tower served as a reception center for Cuban refugees who arrived in Miami between 1962 and 1974.

Location: 600 Biscayne Boulevard

The *American Police Hall of Fame and Museum* has over 10,000 items on display and is a fascinating stop for those who are seriously interested in law enforcement. Tours are available with advance reservations.

Location: 3801 Biscayne Blvd.
Hours: Daily 9–4
Fees: Adults $3, seniors and children $1.50
Phone: (305) 573–0700

For an unusual musical experience, go to the *Miami Marine Stadium.* It was designed to meet its audience on land and sea! Watch a concert from the grandstand in the traditional way or watch and listen from your boat. Views and sound are excellent from both locations.

Location: 3601 Rickenbacker Causeway

Phone: (305) 361–6730 for show information

Sailboats in the Harbor, Miami

Little Havana is Miami's Latin Quarter and Calle Ocho is its main street. Drive along Calle Ocho until you find "your" stop for a cup of strong Cuban coffee, some shopping, and an opportunity to practice your Spanish and appreciate the diversity of the city.

Days filled with sightseeing could easily be spent in Miami. However, it is now time to move on to Miami Beach, the second of the Miami Seven.

Miami Beach

Carl Fisher, a masterful developer, made Miami Beach his city. He understood the development opportunity that would occur if he converted what was a sandspit into an international resort. Mr. Fisher was a master promoter. In 1919, he used elephants to 'elephant–doze' Miami Beach into being from the mangrove forested sandspur.

The Art Deco District stretches from 6th to 23rd Streets. It contains over 800 buildings, built from the 1920s to the 1940s and designed in the Art Deco style. In one sense, these buildings

are large–scale sculptures. In total, they represent the largest remaining collection of Art Moderne/Art Deco structures in America. Tours are available and are highly recommended. This area is the only National Historic District which has been built in the 20th century. *Ocean Drive*, between 6th and 13th Streets, comes alive each evening with outdoor cafes and music from many eras and cultures.

Art Deco District, Miami Beach

Location:	Leslie Hotel, Ocean Drive
Hours:	**Tours:** Saturday at 10:30.
Fees:	**Tour:** $5
Phone:	(305) 672–2014

The *Bass Museum of Art* is noted for its Oriental bronzes as well as its 14th to 20th century European paintings, sculpture, textiles, and decorative arts. If your time is limited, go right to the rare collection of 16th century tapestries. They are exceptional.

Location:	2121 Park Avenue
Hours:	Tuesday through Saturday 10–5, Sunday 1–5, closed Mondays and holidays
Fees:	Adults $2, students $1, no charge on Tuesday
Phone:	(305) 673–7530

North Miami

Be prepared, for the next stop is beyond all expectation. You are about to visit the oldest reconstructed building in the Western hemisphere.

The *Monastery of St. Bernard (also known as the Ancient Spanish Monastery)* was built by slaves near Zamora, Spain in 1141 AD. It was reconstructed on these premises about 40 years ago. Look carefully and you can see the stonemason's symbols which were carved into the rock in the 12th century. There is the Star of David used by Jewish slave workers, the Crescent carved by the Moorish slaves, and the Cross carved by Christian slaves.

The story of its arrival in North Miami bears telling. We've already discussed some of the opulent mansions built in Florida. William Randolph Hearst was also shopping in Europe for important additions to his California estate, San Simeon. He saw the Monastery of St. Bernard and purchased the entire structure as it stood in Zamora, Spain. It was dismantled, packed, and shipped to the United States where it only needed to clear customs in order to be on its way to California and reassembly.

Unfortunately each stone was not numbered during dismantling. The only numbering done was to identify the order in which the more than 10,000 crates were to be reassembled. When the crates arrived at U.S. Customs, a serious problem was noted. The stones had been protected by straw. Straw was not on the approved packing materials list and it was not allowed to enter the U.S. Each crate had to be opened, each stone had to be taken out. All of the straw was destroyed. The stones were then reloaded into the crates.

The stones were not reloaded according to any particular order. Mr. Hearst felt the reassembly task would be monumental. He lost interest and did not accept the shipment.

For many years the crates gathered dust in New York Customs warehouses. Finally, about 40 years ago several Florida men purchased all the crates. They had the reassembly done. The

Monastery is well worth seeing—particularly considering all of its history! A visit to this historic site is enhanced by a look at the formal gardens.

Location:	West Dixie Highway at 167th Street Northeast
Hours:	Monday through Saturday 10–5, Sunday 12–5, closed Easter, Thanksgiving and Christmas
Fees:	Adults $4, seniors (over 65) $2.50, children 6–12 $1
Phone:	(305) 945–1461

Key Biscayne

Bill Baggs Cape Florida State Park and The Cape Florida Lighthouse. This lighthouse was another in the line of safety nets along the Eastern Coast. Climb its 100+ steps for a breathtaking view and imagine standing there watching ships on the horizon racing against an approaching storm. In the 1830s Seminole Indians trapped the keeper and his assistant in the tower. The lighthouse keeper threw a keg of explosives from the top of the building. The explosion was heard by a passing patrol ship and the keeper and his assistant were rescued. This may be one of the few cases on record where a boat saved a lighthouse and its keeper. Be sure to visit the keeper's home while you're on the property.

Location:	1200 South Crandon Boulevard
Hours:	Daily 8–sunset. Lighthouse tours offered
Fees:	$3.25 per vehicle, maximum of 8 people per car
	Admission to lighthouse $1

Coconut Grove

Coconut Grove began as a winter resort in the late 1800s. Commodore Ralph Middleton Monroe (a photographer, naval architect, and builder of shallow draft boats) was largely responsible for its emergence as an artistic and cultural center. In 1882, Commodore Monroe encouraged Charles and Isabella Peacock to build the first hotel on the South Florida mainland. *The Grove*, as the area became known, developed into a spirited, diversified community. It attracted New England intellectuals, Key West Conchs, Bahamians, other year–round residents, and winter visitors.

Commodore Monroe named his home *The Barnacles*. It now serves as the centerpiece of the *Barnacle State Historic Site* providing a fine introduction to how the area looked before Miami's large–scale development occurred in the 1920s and 1930s. Since the Commodore built boats, he was particularly interested in the efficient use of space. As you tour the house, notice the practicality of how he designed the furniture and fittings.

Location:	3485 Main Highway
Hours:	Tours: Thursday through Monday at 10, 11:30, 1 and 2:30. Tours are limited to 10 people on a first–come, first–served basis
Fees:	General admission $2
Phone:	(305) 448–9445

Opened in 1938, the *Fairchild Tropical Garden* is the largest botanical garden in the continental U.S. It includes lakes, pools, and about 5,000 different plant varieties. Whether you're a serious botanist, or simply interested in a beautiful stroll, plan to spend some time here. Tram tours and a guided walking tour are also available.

Location:	10901 Old Cutler Road
Hours:	Daily 9:30–4:30, closed Christmas
Fees:	Adults $4, no charge for children under 13
Phone:	(305) 667–1651

Coral Gables

George Merrick planned a master suburb. Take a bicycle ride or a slow drive through this community to appreciate the elaborate detail involved in its overall land use plan.

Within the 12–mile square city, Mr. Merrick incorporated a Mediterranean community, a walled–in South African compound, and a section of Dutch– and Chinese–inspired residences. The results are interesting and imaginative, particularly since he had never visited any of these countries.

When he began designing the area, there was a large, somewhat ugly, limestone quarry just where he wanted the entrance to the community. He finally came up with the perfect solution: the *Venetian Pool*. With its bold conversion into a large tropical pool with an attached Venetian building, his design problem was erased. A beautiful and ornate entrance to the community occurred and a recreational facility was created. When you look at the pool, realize that until 1986 the pool was drained daily. It was often used as an amphitheater for evening performances.

Location: 2701 DeSoto Boulevard

Stop at the *City Hall*, built between 1927–1928. It is a good example of Mr. Merrick's interpretation of Mediterranean revival architecture.

Location: 405 Biltmore Way

George Merrick's boyhood home is now the *Coral Gables House*. Its original 1898 board and batten construction remains, as does the 1906 addition of locally quarried coral rock. It has been restored to represent Coral Gables architecture and room settings as they would have been at the turn of the century.

Location: 907 Coral Way
Hours: Daily 10–5
Fees: Adults $1, children 50¢
Phone: (305) 460–5360

Hurricanes are taken very seriously in Florida. When a major storm is in the area, we recognize the important work of the *National Hurricane Center*. Guided tours can be arranged if you would like to learn more about this important resource as well as how to prepare for and track major storms. Phone ahead to make tour arrangements.

Location: 1320 South Dixie Highway
Hours: Weekdays 9–4, with appointments
Fees: No charge
Phone: (305) 666–4612

The *Lowe Art Museum* houses the Kress Italian Renaissance and Baroque art collection, the Cintas Foundation's Spanish master paintings, and art of Asia.

Location:	1301 Stanford Drive on the University of Miami's Coral Gables Campus
Hours:	Tuesday through Saturday 10–5, Sunday 12–5, closed July 4, Thanksgiving, Christmas, and New Year's Day
Fees:	Adults $4, seniors (over 65) and students with ID $2
Phone:	(305) 284–3535

South Miami

The *Miami Metrozoo* is a 290–acre facility that provides visitors the opportunity to see exotic animals in their natural habitats. The animals are uncaged, the visitors are protected and the monorail trip is a must. There are three animal shows daily—try to arrange your visit to see at least one of them. The zoo is one of only a few in the U.S. featuring a prominent Koala exhibit. Another highlight is the African Plains section where one can observe the elegant Grevy zebra.

Zebra at the Miami Metrozoo

Location: 12400 Southwest 152nd Street
Hours: Daily 9:30–5:30
Fees: Adults $8.25, children 3–12 $4.25
Phone: (305) 251–0400

It is always fun to look at a site from the water. The *Charles Deering Estate* is located on a 360–acre site on Biscayne Bay. It is now a county park. If your time is limited, plan to take the unusual and imaginative floating tour. Canoes are provided for a small fee, so don't bring your own. With a little more time, tour the two historic homes on the property and hike the trails into the mangrove forest.

Location: 16701 Southwest 72nd Avenue
Hours: Saturday and Sunday 9–5, Canoe tours at 9:30 and
                 1
Fees: **Park**: Adults $4, children $2. **Canoe and grounds:**
                 Adults $10, children $5
Phone: (305) 235–1668

The *Weeks Air Museum* is dedicated to the preservation and restoration of aircraft. The collection includes planes from the beginning of flight to the end of World War II. Most of the aircraft are maintained in flying condition.

Location: 14710 Southwest 128th Street
Hours: Daily 10–5, closed Thanksgiving and Christmas
Fees: Adults $5, seniors (over 65) $4, children 2–12 $3
Phone: (305) 233–5197

Homestead O
Florida City O

Tour 8.
River
of
Grass

The River of Grass Tour provides the opportunity to observe and learn about nature and yourself. Before beginning the trip, read *The Everglades, River of Grass*, by Marjory Stoneman Douglas. She shares her comments and concerns about the importance of the natural environment. Her work serves as an important example of how to help insure the continuation of this national treasure.

Within the Everglades National Park it is easy to forget time when observing migratory birds, the ever changing river of grass, and the natural environment.

The next stop leads underwater where the same feeling of the immensity of the natural environment and the importance of preserving it persists. The Biscayne National Underwater Park is an exceptionally beautiful environment for observing underseas creatures.

Be careful. The River of Grass Tour is not for the casual visitor. The mystery and beauty of what you experience will be with you forever.

Homestead

Homestead was developed by Henry Flagler to provide housing for his employees and their families as the Miami to Key West portion of the East Coast Railroad was being built.

During the 1930s, there was a great deal of concern for the preservation of the Everglades, one of Florida's natural wonders. In 1934, Congress accepted the state's proposal and over 2,000 square miles of land were set aside. In 1947 when the *Everglades*

National Park was finally created, the area was set at 1,400,533 acres. Of this acreage, about half is land, half is water.

The Everglades is the largest remaining subtropical wilderness in the country. Although comparatives can be discussed, the key to the Everglades is its constantly changing nature. At its core, the Everglades is a slowly moving river of grass over 50 miles wide and only inches deep. As you travel, watch for birds and wildlife. The sky's changing patterns and reflections serve as the backdrop to this magnificent natural environment.

Watch for signs to the main Visitor Center. While there, make arrangements to attend one of the Park Ranger talks and take a tram or sightseeing boat trip. Realizing that this is Florida, be prepared for storms, mosquitoes, and high humidity—particularly if you travel during the summer months. For these reasons, visitors should consider making their first Everglades visit during the Autumn, Winter, or Spring months. Your visit will be enhanced by bringing a birding book and binoculars.

Be alert as you travel and stay on the marked routes. The wildlife here is to be taken very, very seriously. That log is probably an alligator.

Each experience in the Everglades is different. Come with a sense of peacefulness and a readiness to learn. You won't be disappointed.

Blue Herons in the Everglades National Park

Location: 12 miles Southwest of Homestead on Route 9336
Hours: Visitor Centers (there are five): Daily 8–5
Fees: $5.00 per vehicle, including riders. $2 per person
on foot, bicycle, etc.
Phone: (813) 695–3311 (this is the ranger station number)

Located in the Everglades, the *Chekika State Recreation Area* has over 100 species of birds, alligators, and otters. When the water table becomes low, be on the lookout for the rare, endangered Florida panther.

Back during the Second Seminole Indian Wars (1839–1840), U.S. Army soldiers set out in 16 canoes to find Chief Chekika's hideaway. It is said that Chekika, a Seminole Chief, had been responsible for several attacks on settlers in the area. The soldiers paddled down Everglades waterways, surprised him here, and killed him. The Chekika Raid marked the first time the U.S. Army moved into an inaccessible area to wage a battle.

Location: Route 27, 11 miles North of Homestead

One of the difficulties when describing national treasures is the use of superlatives. So, let it simply be said that the *Biscayne National Underwater Park* is magnificent! There are more than 180,000 acres of islands and reefs to explore. Of particular interest is the *Offshore Reefs Archaeological District*, where hard and soft coral extend for more than 30 miles in a North–South direction and four to seven miles in an East–West direction.

While at the Park, there is always the possibility of locating a treasure from one of the over 40 shipwrecks in the area. Scuba diving and snorkeling equipment can be rented. Even if you are not interested in being in the water, the glass–bottomed boat tour should be experienced.

Location: For tours: East end of Southwest 328th Street
Hours: Tour arrangements: Daily 8–6
Fees: Three–hour glass–bottomed boat tour: Adults
$14.50, children $8. Four hour snorkel and scuba
diving tour: Adults $21.50 for snorkeling (gear is
provided), $30 for scuba diving, bring your own
gear
Phone: (305) 247–2400

For over 20 years, Edward Leedskalnin collected and carved coral. He used over 1,000 tons of it in fashioning his *Coral Castle* with its hand–hewn furniture, sundial, solar heated bathtubs, and precisely balanced coral gate.

Location:	28655 South Federal Highway (US 1)
Hours:	Daily 9–9
Fees:	Tour: Adults $7.75, children 6–12 $4.50
Phone:	(305) 248–6344

Florida City

We've talked about Mr. Flagler's railroad as the tours have moved down the Florida coast. Florida City was the railroad's last stop before heading over water to Key West and connecting with a boat train to Havana.

Pioneer family life, agriculture, and railroad memorabilia are featured at the *Florida Pioneer Museum.* Built in 1904, the museum is housed in the old Homestead Florida East Coast Railway Depot and Station Agent's House.

Location:	826 North Krome Avenue
Hours:	October through May, Daily 1–5
Fees:	Adults $3, children $1.50
Phone:	(305) 246–9531

Because of its long growing season, Florida has excelled in providing the nation with food. Although citrus crops are best known, the variety of field and tree crops is significant. The *Florida State Farmer's Market* lies in the heart of Florida's fruit and vegetable growing country.

An excellent three–hour tour provides an introduction to the Farmer's Market and a bus tour to farms in the area.

Location:	300 North Krome Avenue
Hours:	**Market:** December–April. **Tours:** December–March at 9 and 1:30, Monday through Friday (phone ahead for reservations)
Fees:	**Tours:** Adults $8, children 12–18 $5
Phone:	(305) 246–6334

We now take mechanized farming for granted. In Florida, as in many other parts of the country, migrant farmers travelled throughout the state bringing in the crops.

Migrant Fruit Picker,
January 1937

An Example of Key West's Tropical Architecture

Key Largo
Islamorada
Indian Key
Big Pine Key   Marathon
Key West

Tour 9.
Hemingway's
Haunts

Expect to be surprised as you drive to the Southernmost tip of the United States along *Florida's Overseas Highway*. It is an engineering marvel that soars from Key to Key across miles of open ocean. The long views of the Gulf of Mexico and the Atlantic Ocean are remarkable, particularly when a storm is brewing. The entire trip is so enjoyable that Key West, one of Ernest Hemingway's haunts, becomes an enchanting bonus.

The Florida Keys

The Florida Keys were sighted around 1513 by Ponce de León. Since there is no record that he or any of his crew came ashore, it is thought that he sailed on and landed farther North.

By the 1700s and 1800s, the location and isolation of the Keys had been noted by many of the fierce pirates working up and down the Eastern Seaboard. They made the Keys hidden shore havens. The Keys became places to store bounty after wrecking ships—or salvaging treasures from ships which had been wrecked during natural storms and hurricanes.

By 1822, the buccaneers had become so brazen that the U.S. Navy Pirate Fleet was established in Key West. These naval men had a tough job. Their mission was to control pirates, pillagers, privateers, and professional wreckers—all of whom thrived in the area. Over time, they were successful.

Almost a century later, Henry Flagler had extended his East Coast Florida Railroad to Miami. Like many visionaries, he turned to the next challenge. Building a railroad from Miami to Key West certainly qualified as a major challenge and the building of the Florida East Coast Railway to Key West began in 1905.

It took seven years to complete the rail extension and it was Mr. Flagler's last railroading project. The extension, difficult enough in its own right, was partially wiped out when hurricanes struck the Keys in 1906, 1909, and 1910. That degree of difficulty should have been seen as an omen of what was to come. However, the natural catastrophes were ignored.

The era of the railway to Key West ended when a major hurricane struck in 1935. The roadbed was so devastated that no attempt was made to repair it . Also, by this time, automobiles and buses were gaining favor as the tourist's way to travel. The next generation of visionaries understood this and went to work. *The Overseas Highway* opened in 1938. It extends for 113 miles and has 43 connecting bridges. For the first time, the entire length of the Florida Keys became easily accessible to residents and travellers.

Key Largo

Lights! Camera! Action!

After Cocoa, this is my favorite town–naming story.

Key Largo was originally known as Rock Harbor. Then came the movies... Several of the interior shots for *Key Largo* were filmed here. After the wonderful Humphry Bogart, Lauren Bacall film came out, the townspeople voted to change the town's name and, in 1952, Key Largo was born.

The first underwater state park in the country is located at the *John Pennekamp Coral Reef State Park*. It covers approximately 70 nautical square miles of coral reefs, seagrass beds, and mangrove swamps. A perfect spot for scuba divers, it is also easy to rent snorkeling gear, or join a snorkeling tour. Make plans for a wonderful day on the water, in the water, or under the water!

Location: Mile Marker 102.5 north of Key Largo
Hours: **Park**: Daily 8–sunset. **Visitor center**: Daily 8–5 **Boat tour**: 9, noon, and 3. Make advance reservations and be there 1 hour before departure
Fees: **Boat tour**: Adults $10 for 9 am trip only; $11 for noon and 3 pm trips, seniors (over 65) $9 for 9 am trip only, children 3–11 $6 for all trips. **Snorkeling tour**: $17 for 9 am tour, $19 for 12 and 3 pm tours
Phone: (305) 451–1202

An Underwater View of Florida

As mentioned earlier in this tour, pirates thrived throughout the Keys for many years. ***Black Caesar's Rock*** (accessible only by boat) is a tiny island. Black Caesar, a Moor, escaped from a slave ship wrecked in the area. He had a business partnership, as it were, with Edward Teach—better known as Blackbeard. Flying the skull and crossbones, their ship, the ***Queen Anne's Revenge***, made a mockery of justice on the seas. Black Caesar and Blackbeard escaped capture for many years. One of their tricks was to race into Black Rock's harbor, have the ship heeled over, and attach it to a huge iron ring so that their potential captors could not see the masts.

During the early 1700s, Black Caesar maintained a prisoner and enemies camp on the island. He was also said to have kept a harem of more than 100 women whom he had captured during his exploits. When he changed islands, the camp was abandoned. Children were left behind to starve. A few survived and developed a primitive language. Seminole legends persisted for many years that the area was haunted by savage creatures. Perhaps those creatures were the adults those children became?

In 1718, the Queen Anne's Revenge was finally captured. Blackbeard was killed during the battle. Black Caesar tried to blow up his ship and all aboard, but failed in the attempt. He was captured, taken to Virginia, and hanged.

Islamorada

Islamorada is a Spanish word meaning Purple Isle. The name refers to the purple snails found in nearby waters.

The Great Hurricane of early September 1935 is commemorated here. The hurricane had winds of 200 miles an hour. A tidal wave more than 12 feet high was driven inland and swept over the Keys. The barometer dropped to 26.35 inches, the lowest sea level reading in the history of the U.S. Weather Bureau. Entire towns were carried out to sea and more than 800 people were killed. Sad to say, few warning signals were given—and most of them were too late.

The Hurricane Memorial reminds us of this tragedy. It includes a large, raised crypt which holds the remains of a few of the World War I veterans who lost their lives. Their story is particularly sad. The veterans had been part of the *Bonus Army*. They had not received money for their unpaid bonus certificates and went to Washington in 1934 demanding payment. Instead, they were offered $30 a month in wages to work on the Overseas Highway. Hundreds of the men were out of work, badly needed the money, and left their families and homes. It is ironic that the hurricane struck on Labor Day 1935. Directly behind the memorial is an 18-foot shaft. At the base is a bronze plaque inscribed with an account of the storm and the toll of lives it took.

Location: 79.9 mile marker
Hours: Daily
Fees: No charge

Indian Key

In the late 1700s, European commercial ships began using the Gulf Stream and the Bahama Channel. These ocean highways were perilously close to then uncharted coral reefs. Ships were often disabled or demolished by the reefs, storms, and hurricanes. The area gained prominence when wrecking and salvage crews found their way to the Florida Keys to take advantage of this entrepreneurial opportunity. If you have access to a boat, it is possible to tour the *Indian Key State Historic Site* and, when you do, think about the following story.

In 1831, Jacob Housman bought the 11-acre island. It became the headquarters for his wrecking business. His company prospered. At one point, there was a permanent settlement of over 60 people, a bowling alley, a hotel, a post office, wharves, and warehouses.

Mr. Housman was greedy and disreputable. In early 1840, he was in the process of negotiating a contract with the U.S. Government which would have permitted him to hunt and kill Indians for $200 a head.

The Seminole Indians learned of these plans and justice was swift. On August 7, 1840, every building in the town, except one, was burned to the ground. The one building spared was the Post Office where a Masonic apron with its mystic symbols was found spread across a table.

Mr. Housman and his family survived the fire. He never reestablished his empire and died in a ship accident six months later.

Today, the Indian Key State Historic Site is wonderful for exploring. Spend a few minutes looking out at the horizon imag–

ining the Seminoles in dugout canoes, the pirate schooners, the brigantines, and the wreckers all passing along the coast.

Location:	One mile West of US 1 at Mile Marker 78.5
Hours:	Thursday through Monday. Three–hour boat tours depart from Indian Key Fill on US 1 at 1:30. On island, 1–hour guided walks are conducted at 10:30, 1 and 2:30. Make reservations early
Fees:	**Boat tour**: Adults and children over 12 $7
Phone:	(305) 664–4815

The San Pedro was a Dutch–built galleon in the New Spain fleet. It left Havana's harbor in July 1773 and sank in these waters. Plan to take a scuba–swim along the underwater nature trail at the *San Pedro Underwater Archaeological Preserve*—a perfect place to go if you have access to a boat and snorkeling gear.

Location:	Oceanside of US 1 at Mile Marker 78.5 (1.3 nautical miles South of Indian Key Island)
Hours:	Daily 8–sunset

Marathon

When the Seven Mile Bridge portion of the Overseas Highway was being built, one of the workers exclaimed that they were involved in a marathon task. The name stuck. The town was named.

Children enjoy a stop at *Crane Point Hammock*. This site combines nature trails, a children's museum, a salt water lagoon, and a wilderness sanctuary.

Location:	Mile Marker 50
Hours:	Monday through Saturday 9–5, Sunday 12–5
Fees:	Adults $4.50, seniors $2.50, students over 12 $1
Phone:	(305) 743–9100

Big Pine Key

One of the best locations for snorkeling in the Keys is at the *Looe Key National Marine Sanctuary*. Expect to feel that you're part of an aquarium as you swim with the tropical fish.

If you scuba dive, there are several wrecked ships, including the 1744 frigate, H.M.S. Looe. Contact local dive shops to make arrangements for tours or diving trips.

Location:	6.7 nautical miles Southwest of Big Pine Key
Phone:	305–872–4039

Key West

Key West is a location and a state of mind. Imagine being in Havana, Cuba in 1822 sitting in a harborside saloon. This is when and where the U.S. Government purchased Key West. Care to guess the purchase price? It was $2,000.

Start your tour in Old Key West. Think about the drive you've taken and the post–pirate environment of the 1880s when the city grew. The architecture is a beautiful blend of Bahamian, Yankee, and Southern. The homes were built or adapted for life in the tropics.

After people decided it was safe to live in Key West, economic growth was rapid. One of the earliest industries in the area was sponge fishing. By 1895 the sponge beds had attracted over 300 boats and 1,400 Greek immigrants.

The Key West Lighthouse Greets Mariners from Land and Sea

The next influx of new settlers came when Cuban immigrants began making cigars here. By 1888, Key West was Florida's largest city and the richest city per capita in America. However, the depression and the 1935 hurricane took their toll on the area. It declined rapidly. The re–emergence has been due to tourism, its tropical climate, its natural beauty, and—at least on the surface— its relaxed life style.

Ernest Hemingway and his wife bought a Spanish colonial house in Key West. Now known as the *Hemingway House and Museum*, the

furnishings reflect the setting in which Papa Hemingway wrote some of his most famous books. Be sure to visit the writing retreat next to the pool. It was here that he composed such works as *A Farewell to Arms, The Snows of Kilimanjaro,* and *For Whom the Bell Tolls.*

Ernest Hemingway at work in Key West

Pick up a copy of *To Have and Have Not* and read Mr. Hemingway's story of rum running between Key West and Cuba. It is a colorful addition to the visual images you will take home after a few days in the area.

The guided tour provides an interesting view of this prolific American writer, his family, and his friends. A word of warning. Stay away if you don't like cats. Mr. Hemingway loved them and had between 50 and 100. Their descendents, at last count 42, are still very much at home on the property. And, if you really like cats, take a moment to count their toes—many have six.

Location:	907 Whitehead Street
Hours:	Daily 9–5
Fees:	Adults $6, children 6–12 $1.50
Phone:	(305) 294–1575

In 1832, John J. Audubon visited Key West. He never lived here. However, the *Audubon House and Gardens* was the first restoration in Key West. The beautiful 19th century home was built for Captain John H. Geiger. Now a museum, it contains a collection of Audubon's engravings as well as fine 18th and 19th century antiques.

John James Audubon. Self-portrait painted in oils when looking in a mirror, 1822

Location:	205 Whitehead Street
Hours:	Daily 9:30–5
Fees:	Adults $5, children 6–12, $1
Phone:	(305) 294–2116

Many artists and writers make Key West home. The *East Martello Museum and Art Gallery* collects the work of Key West authors. Be sure to visit the Key West Authors' Room which is filled with books, photos, and other wonderful treasures. The museum is housed in a brick Civil War fortress fronting the ocean. There is a vast collection of historical artifacts and exhibits which trace Key West's history.

Location:	3501 South Roosevelt Boulevard
Hours:	Daily 9:30–5, closed Christmas
Fees:	Adults $3, children $1
Phone:	(305) 296–3913

People on the Keys take hurricanes seriously. The small *Hurricane Museum* tells about some famous storms, shows what causes a hurricane to happen, and outlines what people should do if they're in a hurricane's path.

Location:	201 William Street
Hours:	Daily 9–5
Fees:	Donations welcome
Phone:	(305) 294–7522

Hundreds of sea life specimens from waters off Key West can be seen at the *Key West Aquarium*. Although it is not necessary to take the guided tour, realize that only those who take the tour can pet the shark. My guess is there may be readers who would avoid the tour in order to miss petting the shark. Don't be one of them.

Location:	One Whitehead Street at Mallory Square
Hours:	Daily 10–6
Fees:	Adults $5.50, seniors (over 55), military personnel, and students $4.50, children 8–15 $2.75
Phone:	(305) 296–2051

The *Key West Lighthouse Museum* commemorates Florida's third oldest brick lighthouse, built in 1847. Climb to the observation level for a sweeping view. Then tour the museum to learn about the lighthouse history of the Florida Keys.

Location:	938 Whitehead Street
Hours:	Daily 9:30–5, closed Christmas
Fees:	Admission to lighthouse or museum: Adults $3, children 7–15 $1
Phone:	(305) 294–0012

The *Wrecker's Museum*, also known as the *Oldest House in Key West,* displays ship models, marine artifacts, and a magnificently furnished doll house of long ago.

Location: 322 Duval Street
Hours: Daily 10–4, closed Christmas
Fees: Adults $2, children 3–12 50¢
Phone: (305) 294–9502

There is nothing subdued about *Sunset at Mallory Square Pier.* Come here to enjoy the people, the street theater, and the sunset. You're sure to have an unforgettable experience, no matter what the weather!

Location: One Whitehead Street

Sunset in a Quieter Setting

93

Central Florida

For many years, Central Florida was noted for the productivity of its citrus groves. However, small, agricultural towns changed rapidly with the arrival of Walt Disney World only little more than 20 years ago. Three tours document the changes.

Tour 10, *Orlando and the Citrus Rim*, highlights the largest city in Central Florida and its Northern communities.

Many people who first come to Florida to enjoy the *Tourist's Mecca* return again and again. West Orange County has become the country's leading tourist destination, with over 30 million visitors vacationing here each year. Tour 11 combines the world class touring with reminders of the ranching era.

The last tour in this section, *Hill Country Adventures,* leads to a college campus with a major collection of Frank Lloyd Wright buildings, visits the highest spot in peninsular Florida to see the gift Edward Bok gave to the state, and stops at Cypress Gardens, the first major theme park in the area.

Florida Citrus Labels

Mount·Dora
Lake Weir
Maitland
ORLANDO
De Land
Sanford
Longwood
Eatonville
Winter·Park

Tour 10. Orlando and the Citrus Rim

Orlando

The town was originally settled by Army volunteers who came to Florida to fight the Seminole Wars and decided to stay.

By the 1870s, the town had become a lawless cattle frontier, not unlike Kissimmee and several other Central Florida areas. Lawlessness reigned for 20 years. By the 1890s, ruined plantation owners from farther North began to arrive, enticed by the climate, water reserves, and relatively inexpensive land. They purchased vast tracts of land for about $1 an acre and began to cultivate citrus groves. As they established families and expanded their businesses, these settlers led Orlando's evolution from a rough frontier town to an expanding community.

Orlando stayed a quiet citrus center until the mid–1960s. Then, changes happened quickly. In a series of secret purchases, the Disney organization bought more than 27,000 acres of land in Orange and Osecola Counties.

Disney's impact continues to be felt throughout the metropolitan Orlando area. Former orange groves have harvested housing developments and office complexes. Orlando became an economically diverse city and attracts major industries in a wide variety of fields.

Three of the area's museums are housed in Loch Haven Park. This is a perfect place to begin an exploration of the city's past. **The Orange County Historical Museum** is a rapidly growing community resource. Be sure to see the pioneer exhibit showing home life on the cattle frontier. There is also an excellent collection of photographs showing Orlando's growth. One of the museum's most popular exhibits is *Fire Station #3*.

Location:	812 East Rollins Avenue
Hours:	Monday through Saturday 9-5, Sunday, 12- 5
Fees:	Adults $2, children 7-12 $1, Monday is donation day
Phone:	(407) 898-8320

The *Orlando Museum of Art* is also located in the Loch Haven complex. Its holdings include a growing permanent collection of 19th and 20th century American art and a fine collection of pre-Columbian artifacts dating from 1200 BC to roughly 1500 AD. The museum also offers a changing series of exhibits and art films.

Location:	2416 North Mills Avenue
Hours:	Tuesday through Friday 9-5; Saturday 10-5, Sunday 12-5
Fees:	Suggested donation: Adults $3; children 6-18 $2
Phone:	(407) 896-4231

Still growing, *The Orlando Science Center and the John Young Planetarium* features hands-on, changing exhibits especially designed for children.

Location:	810 East Rollins Street
Hours:	Monday through Thursday 9-5, Saturday 12-9, Sunday 12-5. **Planetarium**: Monday through Saturday at 11 and 2, Sunday at 2 and 4. **Observatory Star Show** : Friday and Saturday at 8, **telescope** at 9 (weather permitting). Closed Thanksgiving and Christmas
Fees:	**Museum:** Adults $5. Seniors and children 4-11 $4 **Planetarium**: $2 all shows, all ages
Phone:	(407) 896-7151

A turn-of-the-century Florida Victorian house serves as the centerpiece of the *Leu Botanical Gardens*. This lovely in-town park provides seasonal exhibits of camellias, azaleas, roses, flowering trees, and orchids. Guided tours through the Leu family homestead provide a glimpse of how one of Orlando's pioneer families lived.

Location:	231 West Packwood Avenue
Hours:	Monday through Friday 10-4:30, Saturday and Sunday 12-4:30, closed major holidays
Fees:	No charge, donations welcome
Phone:	(407) 539-2181

Longwood

Although North Carolina and Alabama also claim to have the oldest giant bald cypress tree in the country, Floridians believe that *The Senator*, at 126 feet tall, 17.5 feet in diameter, and 47 feet in circumference really holds the record. It is estimated to be about 3,500 years of age. Rows of younger cypress trees stand in a circle around The Senator and provide a fitting honor guard. This is a good place to picnic, quietly give homage to one of Florida's treasures, and reflect upon the changes that have happened on the land since the tree took root.

Location:	Big Tree Park, General Hutchinson Parkway off Highway 17-92
Hours:	Daily, 8 am to sunset
Fees:	No charge

Sanford

In 1871, General Henry R. Sanford, former U.S. Minister to Belgium, bought 12,000 acres of land here. Unable to obtain labor to clear the land and plant citrus groves, he sent an agent to Sweden. The agent recruited 100 workers by offering them passage, all expenses, and a five–acre grove in return for a year's work. Thus began the Swedish settlement in the area.

The *Central Florida Zoological Park* has hundreds of native and exotic animals. The newest additions are the kookaburra and jaguarundi exhibits.

Location:	3755 Highway 17-92 and I-4 (exit 52)
Hours:	Daily, 10-5:30
Fees:	Adults $5, seniors (over 60) $3, children 3-12 $2
Phone:	(407) 323-4450

Lake Weir

As you drive through quiet Lake Weir, realize that in 1935 it was a gangster's lair. Fifteen FBI agents approached a cottage and emptied a small hardware store's stock of bullets into this tiny house. They had been hunting Ma Barker. They killed her in the shootout and stopped her gang which had been robbing, terrorizing, and killing citizens across the country. *Ma Barker's Bullet-ridden Lakeside Cottage* then became a private residence.

Mount Dora

Sailing, antiquing, and sightseeing are among the charms of this 19th century town. Go exploring and find *The Donnelly House,* built in 1893 by one of the town's first promoters and its first mayor. It is one of the best examples of Steamboat Gothic architecture remaining in Florida. Also, be sure to find the Chamber of Commerce office housed in an early railroad depot and, just up the street, pause for tea in a traditional English tearoom.

DeLand

Henry A. DeLand, baking powder manufacturer, founded the community in 1876. In 1889, Lue Gim Gong moved here. His mother had taught him ancient Chinese horticultural methods which he used to perfect and introduce a new variety of orange. By 1892, he had perfected the Gim Gong grapefruit which withstood 10 degrees greater cold than other varieties developed to that time. His contributions were immeasurable to the emerging citrus field.

Stetson University is a good destination for a walk. The *Gillespie Museum of Minerals* houses the second largest private collection of minerals in the world. Be sure to see the 130–pound topaz and take the self guided tour.

Location:	234 East Michigan Avenue, Stetson University
Hours:	Monday through Saturday 9-4, closed National and University holidays
Fees:	No charge
Phone:	(904) 734-4121

ORLANDO ● St. Cloud
Lake Buena Vista Kissimmee

When most first–time tourists arrive in the Orlando area, they head straight to the Tourist's Mecca.

The area is unlike anything else on earth. There are world–class attractions, amusements, animal and aquatic parks, hotels, restaurants, and recreational facilities. The heart of the area's attractions are located in West Orange County and most of the tour is focused on this area. However, Kissimmee and St. Cloud add an opportunity to show how the area is today, as well as how it evolved.

Lake Buena Vista

Only a little more than 20 years ago, Lake Buena Vista was a tiny crossroads town in the midst of woodlands, wetlands, and orange groves. It is now the host community for Walt Disney World. There is so much to do that —given the time, the stamina, and the resources—one could easily spend a week without leaving Walt Disney World.

Within this section, the approach is not to guide you through every activity. Rather, it is to highlight some of my favorite things to see and do. When you arrive on Disney property, ask for a map and an outline of the hours, shows, and special activities at each park. There are well marked and very well staffed guest service areas at each park, at each Disney hotel on the property, and at the Disney Village. Take a few minutes to consider what you want to do first and then prepare for fun, adventure, and surprises.

Four recommendations are offered to help maximize your enjoyment of the parks. First, if you arrive as the doors open, head for the farthest point and work your way back toward the entrance. You'll miss some crowds this way. Second, accept lines as part of the overall experience. Use your time for people watching, tee shirt reading, solving the world's problems, or whatever. Lines move quickly and are almost always shorter than the wait times posted. Third, take a break in the early afternoon for a swim, a meal, or a nap. Consider the two–to three–hour break as a re–energizing stop. The pause is particularly important if you are travelling with children. Fourth, plan to return to the parks in the late afternoon and stay through the evening.

See as many of the evening events as possible—they are marvelous! Our order of preference is IllumiNations, the fireworks and laser show at EPCOT, the Spectro–Magic Parade at the Magic Kingdom, and the Fantasia Fireworks Show at the Disney–MGM Studios.

The newest facility is the *Disney–MGM Studios Theme Park*. It combines movie–related tours, rides, and adventures with working movie and TV studios and larger–than–life–size outdoor sets. If your time here is limited, the following are five of our all–time favorites.

The *Great Movie Ride* provides an animated review of the development of movies in America. It will bring back memories of old classics, legendary stars, and recent thrillers! Robin Williams and Walter Cronkite serve as the improbable hosts for the extraordinary *Animation Tour* which shares the development of animation and gives you the chance to watch Disney animators at work on current projects. *The Backstage Tour* leads you behind the scenes at the working studio! *Star Tours* combines flight simulator technology with laser graphics and a chance to do a little space travelling. One of the newest attractions is the *Muppets 3–D Show*. If you think you understand the limitations of 3–D, see this show twice. Its innovations are outstanding!

By now there's a good chance that you're getting ready for a rest. Consider a Hollywood–style meal at the *Brown Derby*— perhaps the original Cobb Salad and a slice of grapefruit cake.

Location:	Disney complex off I–4 West of Orlando
Hours:	Daily 9–7 (later during some seasons)
Fees:	Adults $33, children 3–9 $26. Ask about discounted fees for multiple day stays and Florida residents
Phone:	(407) W–DISNEY

Consider taking the launch from the Studios to the Yacht Club. Turn right and take a 10– to 15–minute walk to the International Gateway entrance to *EPCOT Center.* The route allows you to enjoy some amazing architecture. It also accesses directly to the *World Showcase.* Make time to see the films, look at the exhibits, meet the Norwegian troll in an action–packed ride, and go shopping at the Chinese and Japanese Pavilions. Realize that the World Showcase is only part of the EPCOT experience. After circling the World, take a launch or bus toward the EPCOT "golf ball." Slowly work your way toward the main entrance, making time for several additional hours of imaginative entertainment. Either leave EPCOT and take a marked bus back to MGM Studios—or return to the World Showcase to see *IllumiNations*, the evening fireworks, fountain, light, laser, and music show. A favorite restaurant for dinner is the outdoor cafe in the French Pavillion. No reservations are accepted. It's a delicious spot for a moderately priced French meal and, if you're really tired, provides a good view of the IllumiNations show while finishing dinner and sipping an iced tea or a glass of wine (French, of course).

Location:	Disney complex off I–4 West of Orlando
Hours:	Daily 9–9 (or later)
Fees:	Adults $33, children 3–9 $26
Phone:	(407) W–DISNEY

The Magic Kingdom is made up of seven lands. Of all the Disney theme parks, this is a fine first stop for children. They meet some of their favorite Disney characters in the area near Cinderella's Castle. Teenagers naturally gravitate to *Space Mountain* and the *Big Thunder Mountain Railroad.* Don't miss *The Haunted Mansion*, the *Pirates of the Caribbean*, and the *Jungle Cruise.*

Two new parades have been introduced. At 3 pm daily, 30– foot–high balloons of Disney figures are the centerpiece of an excellent music and motion parade. In the evening, *Spectro–*

Magic uses fibre optics and ministrobes to light the floats, creating visual surprises throughout the parade!

Location:	Disney complex off I–4 West of Orlando
Hours:	Daily 9–7 (or later)
Fees:	Adults $33, children from 3–9 $26
Phone:	(407) W–DISNEY

First time visitors often limit their Disney adventure to the theme parks. There is much more to see and do. Please read on.

The Nature Preserve

Rarely crowded, *Discovery Island* is an 11–acre island haven for birds, mammals, reptiles, and people. Take a launch from the Magic Kingdom or Fort Wilderness and spend a relaxing few hours following the nature trail.

Location:	Disney complex off I–4 West of Orlando
Hours:	Daily 10–5:30
Fees:	Adults $8, children 3–9 $4.50
Phone:	(407) W–DISNEY

The Water Park

If the day is hot and you're ready for another kind of Disney experience, try *Typhoon Lagoon.* The family–oriented water theme park has frightening white water raft rides for teenagers, a little kids' area with pint–sized water games, and a drifting, lazy river inner–tube float for all ages. Beach chairs, sand, and the giant wave maker provide a good alternative for hot weather enjoyment.

Location:	Disney Complex off I–4 West of Orlando
Hours:	Daily 10–5
Fees:	Adults $18.55, children $14.75
Phone:	(407) W–DISNEY

Evening Attraction

For some people, a full day at the parks is only the beginning. *Pleasure Island* is just plain fun for adults and older children. There is the *Comedy Warehouse*, the *Adventurer's*

Club, the *Neon Armadillo* (a country and western club), dancing, an outdoor bandstand and—as if all that isn't enough—every night is New Year's Eve with a countdown, fireworks, confetti, and the works! Bring your dancing shoes.

Location:	Disney complex West of Orlando
Hours:	Daily 7 pm to 2 am
Fees:	After 7 pm, $12.65 for all. Valid ID required for persons over 18, parent or guardian must accompany anyone under 18
Phone:	(407) W–DISNEY

Office Architecture

Disney continues to make major architectural statements and, over the past several years, has been particularly committed to post–Modernism. Watch for the two new office buildings between Disney Village and Pleasure Island. *Team Disney*, designed by Arato Isozaki, is partially Bauhaus, partially Cubist, and uniquely Disney. Step inside to enjoy space well used and to look at the world's largest sundial. The *Casting Center* is imaginative in a more whimsical way. Particularly notice the details outside the building and along the corridor leading to the reception center.

Hotel Architecture

Disney hotels are part of the wraparound destination resort experience. Properties range from luxurious to whimsical. The always elegant *Grand Floridian* is particularly beautiful during the Christmas season. A special afternoon pause is *High Tea* served just beyond the main lobby.

The *Yacht and Beach Clubs* provide a setting of subdued, beachside elegance and are located just a few minutes away from EPCOT. Designed by Robert A. M. Stern, pay particular attention to the finishing details used throughout the buildings. Nearby are two hotels designed by Michael Graves: *The Swan* and *The Dolphin*. The exteriors and interiors are unexpected and particularly interesting to see when accompanied by children. Listen for and enjoy their reactions as they discover the features.

Also in the Lake Buena Vista Area

The *Hyatt Regency Grand Cypress* is a world–class hotel. Located near the Disney property, it combines convenience to the theme parks with quiet elegance. Sunday is a good time to visit and enjoy brunch. After dining, you'll probably need to take a walk. Although there is a fitness trail, a leisurely stroll around the pool and through the gardens is recommended. Any day is a fine time to tour the convention, reception, and garden areas to look at the impressive Asian, European, and American art and sculpture.

Location:	60 Grand Cypress Boulevard
Phone:	(407) 239–1234

Just a short distance from the Grand Cypress is a treasure of another kind. *Mel Fisher's World of Treasure* shows part of the collection Mr. Fisher and his crew recovered in July 1985. That treasure had been in the Atlantic off the Florida coast since September 4, 1622.

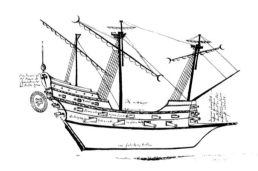

A sketch of a Spanish Galleon done by an English Spy, ca. 1588

On that day, a fleet of 22 treasure–laden Spanish galleons left Havana harbor bound for Spain. They were all blown off course and wrecked near Sebastian Inlet during a hurricane. A second fleet of 11 Spanish galleons left Havana on July 24, 1715, almost a century later. Like their predecesors, they were also blown off course and wrecked off the Sebastian coast. The story of the Fisher treasure search, the story of the find, and the actual treasures are here to enjoy.

Location:	8586 Palm Parkway (at Vista Center)
Hours:	Daily 10 am to 11 pm
Fees:	Adults $6.95 , seniors and children $4.95
Phone:	(407) 239–6000

Kissimmee

The Calusa Indian name for what is now Kissimmee was *Heaven's Place*. Although white settlement to the area began in 1878, it was the arrival of Hamilton Disston which would change the area's future. On the surface, it was simple enough. In 1880, Mr. Disston, a millionaire from Philadelphia, came to Florida to fish on East Tohopekaliga Lake. William Bloxham, Florida's Governor at the time, invited himself along on the fishing outing. The Governor knew Mr. Disston was interested in Florida real estate and Florida was broke. They fished, they talked, and they struck a deal.

A year later, the State of Florida sold Mr. Disston and his partners four million acres of land for 25¢ an acre. The land extended from North of Tarpon Springs on the West Coast to more than halfway across Central Florida, and as far South as Lake Okeechobee. Think of its value a hundred years later!

The land purchase served three important purposes for the state. It replenished a flat treasury, it attracted monied investors' attention to Florida's real estate, and it emphasized the state's interest in developing its land. The precedent for land deals in return for development opened the way for other entrepreneurs.

Mr. Disston and his associates cleared and drained land, created canals, and began the development process. Unfortunately, Mr. Disston died before realizing the great financial benefits his farsighted negotiations and investment caused to happen.

It is interesting to note that seven years after Mr. Disston arrived, a young family bought an orange grove near Kissimmee. Their names were Flora and Elias Disney. A few years later they moved to Chicago where Walter Elias Disney was born.

Also known as Cow Town, Kissimmee has had a colorful history. In 1895, Frederic Remington arrived to sketch, sculpt, and draw the cattlemen. He was not impressed. In sharp lines, he etched the portrait of a Cracker cowboy. As he later told his story, Kissimmee was a frontier town that was so wild that even seasoned ranchers stayed safely inside at night.

Today, the community serves two publics. On one hand, it continues to serve as the regional trading center for the area's ranching operations. It also is one of the largest tourist support areas in the country.

The *Flying Tigers Warbird Air Museum* is dedicated to restoring World War II aircraft to flying condition. Since many of the planes are privately owned, the collection on display is constantly changing. Retired servicemen who know and love airplanes and aviation history serve as guides for an interesting 45–minute tour.

Location:	231 North Airport Road
Hours:	Daily 9–5:30, closed Christmas Day
Fees:	Adults $6, seniors (over 60) and children 6–12 $5
Phone:	(407) 933–1942

Have you wondered how Tupperware is manufactured, how food storage evolved from the Egyptian era, or what is behind the Tupperware Parties? Come to the *Museum of Historic Containers* at *Tupperware World Headquarters* where these questions are answered. As you take the self–guided tour, it's interesting to realize that Tupperware products are sold in over 40 countries and that a Tupperware party happens somewhere in the world every 2.7 seconds. Before leaving take a second look at the headquarters building which was designed by Edward Durrell Stone.

Location:	2175 North Orange Blossom Trail (US 441 south of the Florida Turnpike and the Beeline)
Hours:	Monday through Friday 9–4
Fees:	No charge
Phone:	(407) 847–3111

One of the largest alligator attractions in Florida is *The Gatorland Zoo*. It combines a working alligator farm, a zoo, gator shows, and a narrow gauge railroad tour. Climb the three– story observation tower and watch as logs in the water become alligators. Alligators are part of life in Florida and this is a fine place to learn more about them.

Location:	14501 South Orange Blossom Trail
Hours:	Labor Day to Memorial Day, Daily 8–7
	Memorial Day to Labor Day, Daily 8–6
Fees:	Adults $6, children 4–11 $4
Phone:	(407) 855–5496

St. Cloud

No matter how much you know about snakes, be prepared to learn more when visiting the *Reptile World Serpentarium*. The facility is one of the world's leading production and distribution centers of snake venom and houses more than 1,500 reptile species from around the world.

Location:	5705 East Bronson Memorial Highway
Hours:	January through August and October through December: Tuesday through Sunday 9–5:30, closed Thanksgiving Weekend and Christmas
Fees:	Adults $3.75, children 6–17 $2.75, children 3–5 $1.75
Phone:	(407) 892–6905

Unincorporated Orange County
Lights, Camera, Action, and Splash

Return to the Tourist's Mecca with a trip along International Drive and Kirkman Road.

Sea World of Florida has several new exhibits. Be sure to see *Terrors of the Deep*, featuring fearsome underwater creatures. The exhibit has multiple aquariums and the visitor feels immersed in the underseas world of eels, sharks, barracudas, sea snakes, and other predators from the deep. Another of our favorite activities is the *Whale and Dolphin Discovery Show*.

Location: 7007 Sea World Drive
Hours: Daily 9–9
Fees: Adults $28.55, children 3–9 $24.30
Phone: (407) 351–3600

Universal Studios Florida is a combination theme park and working sound stages and sets for TV and movie production. There are outstanding attractions. A few of our favorite rides include the following. The **Back to the Future Ride** is the most technically sophisticated theme park ride we've seen. It is bumpy, adventuresome, imaginative, and not recommended for people with weak stomachs. If you do take the ride, you will probably want to get in line for a second ride to try to try to figure out how all of those wonderful effects happened. Also be sure to experience *Earthquake* and *Psycho*. Other favorite attractions are the *Wild West Stunt Show*—and the *Animal Show*. This location demands a full day. Go early, take a break in the afternoon, and return for more touring, a slow walk through the lifelike sets, and the evening stunt show on the lagoon. There is a *Hard Rock Cafe* on the property which was built to resemble a guitar—when seen from the air.

Location: 1000 Universal Studios Plaza, off Kirkman Road
                 near the intersection of I–4 and Florida's Turnpike
Hours: Daily 9 am–10:30 pm
Fees: Adults $29, children 3–11 $23; there are also mul-
                 tiple day passes and annual passes
Phone: (407) 363–8000

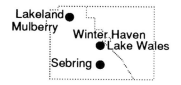

Lakeland●
Mulberry Winter Haven
●Lake Wales
Sebring ●

Tour 12.
Hill
Country
Adventures

Fasten your seat belt! Tour 12 travels along the highest land in peninsular Florida. A major statement is made when we must say that the highest point of land is just over 300 feet above sea level.

Lakeland

Lakeland's contemporary history began with the coming of the South Florida Railroad in 1884. Henry Plant worked to establish a railway system on the West Coast during the same period that Henry Flagler was building his railway on the East Coast. Lakeland serves as a trading center for the agricultural and mining communities nearby.

Frank Lloyd Wright came to Florida in 1938 at the request of a college administrator at *Florida Southern College*. For over 20 years, he worked to develop the *Child of the Sun Collection* of buildings on the campus. Twelve structures create the largest one–site concentration of Mr. Wright's work in the world. Following his death in 1959, Nils Schweizer, his student and protege, continued work on the campus by designing several structures which continue the feel of the Wright buildings.

A self–guided tour brochure is available. If you plan your visit when school is in session, step inside the Administration Building to see examples of Mr. Wright's designs in decorative arts and furnishings. Another good time to visit is on a Sunday morning to see the *Annie Pfeiffer Chapel*, one of the buildings he designed. Go to the second level and look through the windows for an overview of the entire collection.

Location:	North Shore of Lake Hollingsworth. Park a block up from the lake on Johnson Street to begin the self–guiding tour.
Hours:	Daily
Fees:	No charge
Phone:	(813) 680–4131

Mulberry

Mulberry was named for a large mulberry tree that grew near the railroad tracks. In the old days, shipments were simply marked, "Put off at the big mulberry tree." Riding through town today, it is difficult to realize that less than a century ago Mulberry was filled with gamblers and outlaws. The town became famous because of its phosphate mines. It looked like a Western gold mining town where saloons, dance halls, and chaos were often the only order of the day.

In 1919, the town became the site of the state's largest labor–management dispute. Over 1,000 miners left the phosphate mines and went on strike. They wanted better working conditions and higher wages. When the strike began, the miners were working 10–12 hours a days and were paid $2.50 a day. Although management eventually broke the strike, an increased wage scale of $3 was put into effect and the work day was shortened to only 8–10 hours a day.

Over half of the world's phosphate is produced in the area. And where there is mining, there is excavation. *The Phosphate Museum* contains bones and fossil artifacts from Florida's prehistoric era. One of the newest finds has been the Baleen whale skeleton, which is over 10 million years old and more than 18 feet long.

Location:	Highway 37 South, just behind the City Hall
Hours:	Tuesday through Saturday 10–4:30
Fees:	No charge
Phone:	(813) 425–2823

Sebring

George Sebring, a pottery manufacturer from Sebring, Ohio, planned the town based on the pattern of the mythological Heliopolis (City of the Sun). Streets radiate from a central park which represents the sun. When Florida's real estate frenzy of 1924–25 began, the town was one of the first to hire an official greeter. He spent his days in the town meeting visitors and promoting Sebring as a great place to live. It worked! If you're interested in car racing, come check out this world–class track.

Lake Wales

Bok Tower and Gardens lift the eyes, refresh the soul, and bring joy to the spirit. Edward Bok was a Norwegian immigrant who became publisher of the **Ladies Home Journal**. In 1923, he bought the ridge land and selected Frederick Law Olmsted, Jr., the eminent landscape architect, to convert the scrub and orange grove into a beautiful sanctuary.

Mr. and Mrs. Bok gave the completed Tower and Gardens to the American people. President Calvin Coolidge joined the Boks to dedicate the site in 1929.

Bok Tower

Before walking through the gardens to the Tower, watch the narrated slide presentation in the *Old Cracker House Visitor Center*. Then walk up the hill to *The Overlook* which is located at the highest point on the property. The valley you see below was part of the ocean floor half a million years ago.

Bok Tower is the centerpiece of the facility. It was constructed of pink and gray Georgia marble and Florida coquina stone. Sculpture covers parts of the tower with Florida's herons, pelicans, flamingos, geese, and swans. The Tower houses a 57–bell carillon which was cast in Loughborough, England. The largest bell, the Bourdon, weighs over 11 tons—the smallest treble weighs 17 pounds.

Although it's not open to the public, the Tower's brass *Creation Door*, with its 30 panels, is particularly impressive. If you could enter the doors, you would find the largest carillon library in the world on one of the upper floors.

If you arrive between November and March, the Garden's camellias are in full bloom. The period between December and April is also particularly impressive for seeing the extensive azalea display.

Location:	3 miles North of Lake Wales off Highway 27
Hours:	Daily 8–5
Fees:	Adults $3
Phone:	(813) 676–1408

We talked about Kissimmee's wild frontier earlier. The *Kissimmee Cow Camp* provides a living–history interpretation of the area's cattle country, circa 1876. The stories of the Florida cowboys are wonderful and you can easily spend an afternoon watching the kids imagine the good old days.

Location:	Camp Mack Road, on the grounds of the Lake Kissimmee State Park
Hours:	Saturday, Sunday, and major holidays 9:30–4:30
Fees:	$3.25 per car, including up to 8 people per vehicle
Phone:	(813) 696–1112

Winter Haven

The granddaddy of all of Florida's outdoor theme parks is *Cypress Gardens.* In the 1930s, Dick Pope, a master tourism promoter for Central Florida, and his family developed the 233 acre center. His aim was to make it a facility where families would have fun together. It is said that Walt Disney took his children there and spent time in the parking lot noticing the large number of out–of–state license plates and the larger numbers of families visiting.

Walkways lead through acres of beautiful, towering cypress trees that provide shade for over 5,000 varieties of flowers and plants. If you do nothing else, make time for the *Botanical Gardens*. They are exceptional. Plan to spend a full day to fully enjoy the variety of attractions and shows—particularly the water skiing.

Mr. Pope did a great deal to promote water activities and water skiing. He attracted Esther Williams to the site, built a swimming pool for her use, and probably helped oversee her films that were produced at Cypress Gardens. Plan to tour the *Water Ski Museum and Hall of Fame* which traces the sport from 1922.

Location:	State Road 540, East of Winter Haven
Hours:	Daily 9–6
Fees:	Adults $18.95, children 3–9 $12.95
Phone:	(813) 324–2111

Winter Haven has been a major citrus producing area in Florida for many years. Try to arrange a visit during the orange blossom season.

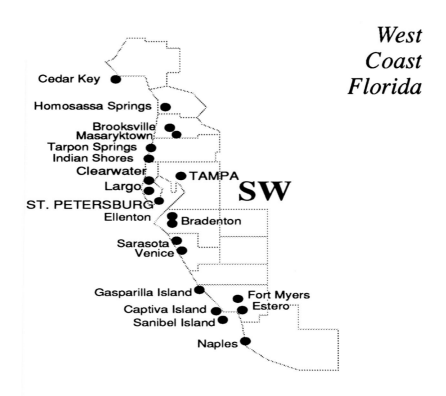

West Coast Florida

Cedar Key

Homosassa Springs

Brooksville
Masaryktown
Tarpon Springs
Indian Shores
Clearwater
Largo
ST. PETERSBURG
Ellenton

●TAMPA

SW

Bradenton

Sarasota
Venice

Gasparilla Island
Captiva Island
Sanibel Island

Fort Myers
Estero

Naples

The communities curving around the West Coast of the Gulf of Mexico are quite different from those you visited along the state's East Coast.

Tampa and St. Petersburg are two major cities in this area. They have a friendly rivalry, cater to different audiences, and serve as a *Dynamic Duo* for business and industry as is described in Tour 13.

The Greatest Show on Earth winters on the West Coast. Take Tour 14 and learn about the Ringlings, the circus, how you can preview new shows, and two of America's greatest inventors.

An entirely different mood prevails along the Northern portion of the West Coast. Time slows down as you drive toward Cedar Key. Enjoy a leisurely drive through hardwood forests as you find the *Time–Lapse Territory* described in Tour 15.

Tour 13.
The Dynamic Duo
Tampa and St. Petersburg

Tampa and St. Petersburg maintain a friendly rivalry. St. Pete combines a beach community with an active business community. Over the past several decades, Tampa has grown rapidly and has emerged as a modern, metropolitan city.

Tampa

Henry B. Plant was as important to Western Florida as William Morrison Flagler was to the East Coast. Mr. Plant extended his railroad and hotel system down the West Coast.

The *Henry B. Plant Museum* is located on the *University of Tampa* campus in the former *Tampa Bay Hotel.*

In 1884, Mr. Plant, a Connecticut industrialist, extended his railroad and shipping system to Tampa. At that time, the city was a small town with 700 residents. Because of his remarkable economic efforts, the population expanded to 5,000 residents by 1890. In that year he opened the opulent Tampa Bay Hotel.

Henry B. Plant

117

The once fashionable winter resort was designed by John A. Wood. It was the first large, fully electrified building in Tampa and was promoted as the world's most elegant hotel.

It was believed that many of the early efforts regarding American involvement in the Spanish–American War began in Ybor City, Tampa's Spanish and Cuban area.

Tampa Bay Hotel , ca. 1890

During the War, some 30,000 troops were encamped in the Tampa–Lakeland area and then Colonel Teddy Roosevelt was often seen riding his horse, Texas, throughout Tampa accompanied by his dog, Cuba.

The hotel served as headquarters for American troops. Look around and think of Colonel Roosevelt training his Rough Riders on the grounds. Nearby, Frederic Remington might have been working on his charcoal sketches.

Teddy Roosevelt and the Rough Riders

Winston Churchill, a young reporter in 1898, stayed at the hotel while covering the War. Clara Barton, founder of the Red Cross, had her headquarters in the city and was preparing to help the injured.

The museum has interesting Victorian era furnishings. However, the building itself is a treasure with its ornate Moorish architecture, domed towers, and bulbous minarets topped with silver crescents. Parking is often difficult, so be prepared to walk.

Location:	401 West Kennedy Boulevard
Hours:	**Museum:** Tuesday through Saturday 10–4. **Campus tour:** September through May, Tuesday and Thursday at 1:30. Museum closed and no tours on Thanksgiving, Christmas and New Year's Day Phone ahead for reservations
Fees:	**Museum:** Adults $2, children 50¢. **Campus tour:** no charge
Phone:	(813) 253–6220

Tampa's Museum of Art has a large permanent collection including Greek and Roman antiquities as well as 19th and 20th century paintings. Be sure to see the photography exhibits and the C. Paul Jennewein Sculpture Collection with over 2,000 pieces. About 30 objects on display on the Museum's Terrace Gallery.

Location:	601 Doyle Carlton Drive
Hours:	Tuesday through Saturday 10–5, Wednesday 10–9, Sunday 1–5, closed major holidays
Fees:	No charge, suggested donation $2
Phone:	(813) 223–8130

Recently opened, make time for the *Museum of African–American Art*. It contains works which date from the 1800s to the present, focusing on a people and a nation. Included are works by Edward Bannister, Romare Bearden, and Henry Tanner.

The museum also houses the Barnett–Aden African–American Art Collection which developed in Washington in the 1940s. Of particular interest is the work of Lois Mailou Jones. Guided tours are provided. Phone ahead to make advance tour reservations.

Location: 1308 North Marion Street
Hours: Tuesday through Saturday, 10–4:30, Sunday 1–
               4:30, closed Easter, Labor Day, Thanksgiving,
               Christmas, and New Year's Day
Fees: No charge, suggested donation $2
Phone: (813) 272-2466

Children enjoy many of the interactive exhibits at the *Museum of Science & Industry*. These exhibits relate to agriculture, environment, industry, and weather. The weather exhibits are particularly interesting as you experience a simulated hurricane and learn about a thunderstorm as part of *Dr. Thunder's Magic Boom Ride.*

Location: 4801 East Fowler Avenue
Hours: Sunday through Thursday 9–4:30, Friday and
               Saturday 9–9, closed Easter, Thanksgiving,
               Christmas, and New Year's Day
Fees: Adults $4, children 5–15 $2
Phone: (813) 985-5531

Busch Gardens is an African theme park with over 3,000 animals ranging from rare white Bengal tigers to African big game. There are giraffes and zebras roaming free on the veldt–like *Serengeti Plain*. Allow a full day for this attraction and be prepared to come back to see even more.

The ice show at the *Moroccan Palace Theatre* is particularly enjoyable on a hot day. The park also includes rides such as *Questor* (a flight simulator experience) and the *Congo River Rapids* white water raft ride.

Location: 3000 East Busch Boulevard at 40th Street
Hours: Daily, 9:30–6
Fees: Adults and children over 2 $25.95
Phone: (813) 987—5082

At the *Lowry Park Zoo* two of our favorite exhibits are the free–flight Aviary and the newly opened *Pepsi Manatee and Aquatic Center*. The center offers emergency care to injured or sick manatees. It is possible to watch their recovery process through large plate glass panels which provide underwater and surface viewing opportunities.

Location:	7530 North Boulevard
Hours:	Winter, daily 9:30–5; summer, daily 9:30–6
Fees:	Adults $5, seniors (over 65) $4, children 3–12 $3
Phone:	(813) 932–0245

Cigar making is big business in Tampa. At *Villazon and Co.* you can see how tobacco is selected as well as how cigars are made and readied for shipment.

Location:	3104 North Armenia Avenue
Hours:	Tour: Monday through Friday at 9:30, closed major holidays and late June through mid–July
Fees:	No charge
Phone:	(813) 879–2291 (phone ahead for tours)

Ybor City

Although Key West was the original Havana cigar capital in America, the Tampa cigar has been famous since the 1880s and was primarily made in Ybor City. During the reign of Alfonso XIII, the old *Cuesta–Rey Cigar Factory* was commissioned as purveyor of handmade cigars to the King and Court of Spain.

Cigar makers, or tabaqueros as they were known, worked at long tables in double rows. While working, readers, or lectors, read to the workers—in the morning it would usually be political tracts; in the afternoon, literature. It was in the cigar factories of Ybor City that the importance of America's involvement in the Spanish–American War was discussed. This ultimately led to letters to the Federal government in Washington, D. C. and the battles that followed.

To learn more about the area's Spanish roots, visit the *Ybor City State Museum*. It is housed in the renovated *Ferlita Bakery*, once a principal source of the community's daily bread. The museum provides a wonderful history of the growth of the area and of the cigar industry in Cuba and Ybor City. The *Cigar Worker's Home* is in the complex and is open for touring.

Location: **Museum**: 1808 9th Avenue. **House**: 1804 9th Avenue

Hours: **Museum**: Tuesday through Saturday 9–12 and 1–5. **Tours** : 10–12 and 1–3

Fees: **Museum**: Adults and children over 6 $1. **Tours**: General admission $1

Phone: (813) 247–6323

The *Ybor Cigar Factory* shows a bit of Florida's heritage. Buildings have been restored and now house a collection of shops and restaurants.

Street Scene, Ybor City

Location: 1901 North 13th Street
Hours: Daily 9:30–9
Fees: No charge to browse
Phone: (813) 247–4497

St. Petersburg

When Mr. Plant's railroad was established in 1885, Peter Demens named the railroad stop after his home city in Russia. During the late 1800s, a medical association emphasized that St. Petersburg was one of the best places to retire, causing a large influx of older citizens. The community is now much more diversified in terms of businesses and ages.

One of the city's best known museums is the *Salvador Dali Museum*. It houses the largest private collection of the famous Spanish surrealist painter's works. The more than 1,000 pieces in the collection date from 1914. They were assembled over a 40–year period by A. Reynolds and Eleanor Morse who wintered in St. Petersburg. Plan to join one of the tours conducted in the gallery and, we expect, you will particularly enjoy learning about the large paintings on the far walls.

Location:	1000 Third Street South
Hours:	**December 26 through Easter:** Tuesday through Saturday 10–5, Sunday and Monday noon–5. **Balance of year:** Tuesday through Saturday 10–5, Sunday noon–5, closed major holidays
Fees:	Adults $5, seniors (over 62) and students $3.50
Phone:	(813) 823–3767

When visiting *The Museum of Fine Arts*, be sure to see the French impressionist paintings. There are also remarkable photography, pre–Columbian, and Steuben glass collections.

Location:	255 Beach Drive, Northeast
Hours:	Tuesday through Saturday 10–5, Sunday 1–5. **Tours** Tuesday through Friday at 10, 11, and 2, Saturday at 11 and 2 and Sunday at 1 and 2, closed Christmas and New Year's Day
Fees:	Suggested donation $4
Phone:	(813) 896–2667

The Pier is a wonderful stop if you're travelling with children. It is a five–story inverted pyramid with a breezy observation deck as well as interesting fresh and salt–water aquariums.

Location:	800 Second Avenue, Northeast
Hours:	Daily 10–9 (aquariums closed on Tuesdays)
Fees:	No charge
Phone:	(813) 821–6164

Go through an 110–foot touch tunnel maze in the dark at the *Great Explorations* hands–on museum. Great for kids!

Location:	1120 Fourth Street South
Hours:	Monday through Saturday 10–5, Sunday noon–5, closed major holidays
Fees:	Adults $4.50, seniors (over 65) $4, children 3–17 $3.50
Phone:	(813) 821–8885

The *St. Petersburg Historical Museum* features thousands of pioneer artifacts showing life of the early Floridians.

Location:	335 Second Ave., Northeast (next to the Pier)
Hours:	Monday through Saturday 10–5, Sunday 1–5, closed Thanksgiving, Christmas and New Year's Day
Fees:	Adults $2, seniors (over 60) $1.50, children 6–11 50¢
Phone:	(813) 894–1052

Four houses are showcased at the *Haas Museum Complex*. The houses date from the 1850s to the 1920s.

Location:	3511 2nd Avenue South
Hours:	Thursday through Sunday 1–5, closed Thanksgiving, Christmas, and New Year's Day
Fees:	Adults $2, seniors (over 62) $1.50 children 6–12 50¢
Phone:	(813) 237–1437

Since St. Petersburg promoted itself as a retirement city for so many years, it is fitting that the world's largest shuffleboard club should be right next to the *Shuffleboard Hall of Fame*.

Experience a trip between St. Petersburg and Sarasota by driving across the *Sunshine Skyway Bridge*. A 4.1– mile span, the bridge is a work of art which crosses Tampa Bay on Highway 275. The design of the suspension bridge catches the light and reminds one of an aerial sailboat.

Sunshine Skyway Bridge

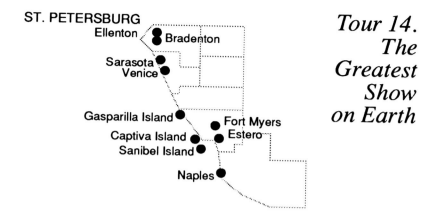

ST. PETERSBURG
Ellenton
Bradenton
Sarasota
Venice
Gasparilla Island
Fort Myers
Captiva Island
Estero
Sanibel Island
Naples

Tour 14.
The
Greatest
Show
on Earth

Allow plenty of time when visiting this beautiful part of the coast. Explorers, plantations, pirates, circus folk, and inventors all await your visit.

The Greatest Show on Earth has its winter headquarters in Venice. The greatest circus couple in America, John and Mable Ringling, built one of America's great palace homes and established a major art museum in nearby Sarasota.

Meanwhile, just down the coast at Fort Myers, Thomas Alva Edison and Henry Ford, two of the greatest inventors of our time, were at work in their laboratories revolutionizing American industry.

Ellenton

Ellenton was a Confederate stronghold during the Civil War. The **Gamble Plantation State Historic Site and Memorial to J. P. Benjamin** is well worth a visit. Formerly a sugar plantation and refinery covering 3,500 acres, it is now the only antebellum plantation that has survived in South Florida. When touring, realize it is representative of many successful mid–19th century plantations that once prospered in the area. Robert Gamble, a banker and Confederate major, built the house in the late 1840s.

Slaves made bricks of broken shell and mortar for the walls. The plaster was a mix of sand, lime, and sugar. Since sugar was raised on the plantation, it was the least expensive binding agent available, and it held very well. In addition to the Plantation house, look at the *Ruins of the Sugar Mill*. At the time of the Civil War, this was one of the largest mills in the South.

Confederate Secretary of State Judah P. Benjamin was sheltered in the plantation house after the fall of the Confederacy. He hid here until safe passage to England could be arranged. The Monument has been erected in his honor.

Location:	3708 Patten Avenue
Hours:	**Park**: Daily 8–sunset. **Tours**: Thursday through Monday at 9:30, 10:30, 1, 2, 3, and 4.
Fees:	**Park**: No charge. **Tours**: Adults $2, children 6–13 $1
Phone:	(813) 722–1017

Bradenton

Life was hard for the early settlers. The *Manatee Village Historical Park* makes it easier to understand the lives of the early Florida pioneers. Six historic buildings were moved to the site and

Early Settlers, ca. 1895

can be toured. They date from 1860 through 1912 and include a courthouse, a church, a farm, a store, a schoolhouse, and a home.

There is an interesting children's hands–on room in the *Wiggins Store* where kids can wear period costumes, play with toys from the early part of the century, and imagine life as a child in those days.

Location:	604 15th Street East
Hours:	Monday through Friday 9–4:30, Sunday 2–5
	Tours: September through May at 9:30–3:30
Fees:	No charge
Phone:	(813) 749–7165

The *De Soto National Monument* commemorates the spot at which de Soto was said to have landed. It includes a 16th century living history camp and visitor center. Make time to see the excellent collection of 16th century European military artifacts. There is also a good reference library relating to this period.

Location:	75th Street Northwest
Hours:	**Visitors Center**: Daily 8–5:30. **History Camp**: December through April 10–5
Fees:	Adults $1, seniors and children under 17, no charge
Phone:	(813) 792–0458

The *South Florida Museum and Bishop Planetarium* tells the story of Florida from prehistoric times to the Space Age. There is a life–size diorama showing how the Indians lived, replicas of de Soto's 16th century Spanish buildings, the Bishop Planetarium, and Snoopy the gentle manatee.

Location:	201 10th Street West
Hours:	**Museum**: Tuesday through Saturday 10–5, Sunday 1–5. **Planetarium**: Tuesday through Sunday at 1:30 and 3 and Friday and Saturday at 7:30. **Laser show**: Friday and Saturday night at 9, 10:30, and midnight; Sunday at 4:30 and 6. **Observatory**: Friday and Saturday from 9–10 pm, weather permitting. **Manatee**: Shown Tuesday–Saturday at 11, 1, 2:30 and 4 and on Sunday at 1, 2:30 and 4. Closed Thanksgiving, Christmas and New Year's Day

| Fees: | **Museum** and **planetarium**: Adults $4, children 5– 12 $1.50. **Laser show**: Adults $4.50, children under 13 $2. **Observatory**: 50¢ |
| Phone: | (813) 746–4132 |

Sarasota

John Ringling, ca. 1905

It is said that John Ringling's flamboyant spirit lives in Sarasota. He made the city the hub of American circusdom. In addition, John and Mable Ringling's outstanding art collection and their generosity to the community established Sarasota as the area's cultural center.

Photo courtesy of Ringling Bros. and Barnum & Bailey Combined Shows, Inc.

By the early 1920s, the circus and some excellent investments permitted the Ringlings to begin designing a residence and museum to house their vast collection. Mr. Ringling had extensive land holdings across Sarasota Bay at Longboat Key. It is particularly fitting that his Florida palace overlooks the Bay and the Key.

The Ringling's mansion is named *Ca'd'Zan*, the House of John. It was built in 1926 and cost $1.5 million—plus furnishings. It clearly ranks as one of the American palaces built during the period. Although the exterior is currently undergoing renovation work, walk to the Sarasota Bay side of the home to appreciate the

Ca' d' Zan

architecture and craftsmanship used throughout. The Ringlings were very much involved in the design of their home and incorporated elements from the Italian and French Renaissance, Baroque, Venetian Gothic, and Modern periods in the architectural design. Look carefully at the period furnishings and art. Then step into the ballroom to note the ceiling panels which were painted by Willy Pogany, set designer for the Ziegfeld Follies.

The John and Mable Ringling Museum of Art, completed in 1929, is known throughout the world for its rich and varied collections including Old Masters, Late Medieval, and Renaissance works. Known as the State Museum of Florida, it and the Louvre share the distinction of owning cartoons and tapestries designed and created by Rubens. Particularly note the *Departure of Lot*, which is believed to have been executed entirely by Rubens.

The John and Mable Ringling Museum of Art

The Four Evangelists, Peter Paul Rubens, Flemish master of the spectacular Baroque style. The Rubens paintings assembled by the Ringlings comprise the greatest and best collection of the artist's work in this hemisphere. This painting was created as one of eleven "cartoons" for tapestries that were woven in Brussels. It is one of four from the same series in the Sarasota museum and one of six still in existence. The other two hang in the Louvre while five were destroyed by fire in 1731. The four Evangelists are seen attended by their Apocalyptic symbols: the lion with St. Mark, the ox with St. Luke, the angel with St. Matthew, and the eagle above St. John holding the Chalice of the Eucharist.

Step right up! Don't miss it! In 1948, two years after assuming ownership of the Museum, the State of Florida honored the Ringlings by establishing the *Circus Galleries*. They take you inside the Big Top and are filled with circus memorabilia. Photographs of circus personalities, rare circus lithographs, posters, and a scale model of a three–ring circus are only a few of the wonderful items you will discover. The *Asolo Theater* is also on the property. It is a restored 19th century Italian theater with ornate panels and an interesting story of its "rediscovery" and purchase.

Location:	US. Highway 41, 3 miles North of downtown
Hours:	**Museums:** Daily 10–5:30 and Thursdays 10–10 (October through June), closed Thanksgiving, Christmas and New Year's Day
Fees:	**Gardens:** no charge. **Buildings: Adults** $8.50, seniors (over 62) $1.50
Phone:	(813) 355–5101

Beauty lives at the *Marie Selby Botanical Garden* which specializes in epiphytes (air plants) from the tropics. The highlight of the visit is a chance to see the outstanding orchid collection. While here, make time to tour the historic *Payne Mansion* which houses the *Museum of Botany and the Arts*.

Location:	811 South Palm Avenue, just off US 41
Hours:	Daily 10–5, closed Christmas
Fees:	Adults and children over 12 $5
Phone:	(813) 366–5730

Sarasota Bay

The *Mote Marine Aquarium* is world renowned for its research on sharks and ongoing studies and assessments of environmental pollutants. The facility also includes a Science Center. There are 22 aquaria containing over 200 varieties of fish and invertebrate sea creatures. Be sure to see the outdoor shark tank. Besides visiting an important aquarium, make a few minutes to enjoy the setting overlooking Sarasota and the Bay.

Location:	1600 City Island Park
Hours:	Daily 10–5, closed major holidays
Fees:	Adults $5, children 6–17, $3
Phone:	(813) 388–2451

Venice

During the land boom of the 1920s, the Brotherhood of Locomotive Engineers came to Florida to find land for a town. John Nolan, an eminent town planner was hired, small farms and residential lots were laid out. Business and industrial districts were also designed to be part of the 30,000–acre plot. Venice was the result. The land boom collapsed in the late 1920s. By 1930, all but a handful of residents had departed.

In the 1960s, Ringling Bros. and Barnum & Bailey Circus selected Venice as its Winter Headquarters. Their arrival has been a major factor in the community's rebirth. Each November the **Greatest Show on Earth** arrives in Venice. Two teams of performers work to design and perfect the two different shows that will be featured during the next season. In late–December star–studded premiers are held in the Venice Arena. As you can imagine, audiences include long term circus fans and former performers who have retired to the area. What a wonderful way to go to the circus! The arena is small, so plan ahead for this exciting circus event.

Location: Venice Arena, 1401 Ringling Drive South
Phone: For show dates and tickets: (813) 483–5145.
For other information call Winter Quarters
(813) 484–9511

Put on a Happy Face. Makeup application is one of the classes taught to fledgling funsters at the Clown College, the only institution in the world solely dedicated to teaching the art of clowning.

Photo courtesy of Ringling Bros. and Barnum & Bailey Combined Shows, Inc.

Ringling Clown College is the most outstanding institution in the world for training performers and others working in the circus. The students learn prop construction, costume fabrication, mime, make–up, juggling, stilts, circus history, and much more. Each year thousands of applicants hope to be among the 60 who will be selected. Although it is not open to the public, the Clown College is part of the complex near the Venice Arena and holds auditions in many towns the circus visits.

North Port

The springs at **Warm Mineral Springs and Cyclorama** produce nine million gallons daily at a constant water temperature of 87 degrees. It is an unexpected treat to cool off here and there is a bathhouse for changing if you decide on a swim. The Cyclorama is a rotunda 226 feet in diameter. It is lined with murals showing Ponce de León's varied and interesting adventures.

Location:	12200 San Servando Avenue
Hours:	Daily 9–5, closed on Christmas
Fees:	Adults $5.75, children 12–18 $3.75, children 2–11 $2
Phone:	(813) 426–1692

Gasparilla Island

In the 1780s, a cultivated, well–dressed, well–read pirate assembled a band of cutthroats. He established a base on an island he named Gasparilla—after himself. Known as José Gaspar when at court in Spain, he renamed himself Gasparilla when he began pirating. In 1801, he captured a Spanish princess, Maria Louisa. A year earlier she had gone to Mexico. She and 11 beautiful, young Mexican noblewomen were sailing to Spain where the Mexican girls were to be educated. Gasparilla struck their vessel off the coast of Boca Grande. He killed the crew, took the gold, and carried the young women off to nearby Captiva Island. He terrorized ship captains and passengers until 1822. In that year, his boat was boarded. Rather than be captured, he tied an anchor around his waist, leaped into the water, and drowned.

Fort Myers

Thomas Alva Edison, 1847–1931. Mr. Edison was one of the most prolific inventors of all time, and held 1,097 patents. He is best known for the invention of the incandescent lamp and the development of the electrical industry. Some of his other inventions created the phonograph, moving picture, telegraph, and telephone industries. Many feel that he is the person who has had the most profound effect on the development of the modern world.

Thomas Alva Edison came to Fort Myers in 1886. He was 39 years old, ill, and trying to regain his health. He succeeded and spent winters in Florida until his death at the age of 84.

While working in his Fort Myers laboratory, Mr. Edison perfected and patented the teletype, the phonograph, motion pictures, and many other inventions. His laboratory, which currently is closed, contains the original equipment used for much of his research from 1925 to 1931.

When he had perfected the electric lamp, Mr. Edison offered to install free lights in the town, provided the residents would supply the poles and wires. The town council rejected the proposal because they felt the lights might keep the cattle awake. Yes, this is serious!

One of Mr. Edison's most treasured gifts was an early Model T given to him by his friend and neighbor, Henry Ford. Each year, it is said, Mr. Ford offered him the new model in exchange for the car and each year the offer was refused. He liked his old car and the fun of owning it.

Mr. Edison and his "Old" Model T

It became quite a tradition at the start of each winter season to see Mr. Ford, his mechanics, and boxes of auto parts arriving at the Fort Myers train station. The new improvements were hand tooled into Mr. Edison's car each year.

You won't be able to miss the giant banyan tree at the entrance to the *Edison Winter Home, Gardens, and Museum*. It was a gift from Henry Firestone in 1928. When planted, it was a few inches in circumference—the circumference is now over 400 feet.

When you look at the Edison home, realize it is one of the earliest prefabs in Florida. Designed by Mr. Edison, it was built in Maine and brought to Fort Myers by schooner in 1886. The furnishings in the home are representative of the early 1900s and the swimming pool is said to be the first residential pool in Florida.

Location:	2350 McGregor Boulevard
Hours:	Monday through Saturday 9–4, Sunday 12:30–4, closed Thanksgiving and Christmas. **Tours:** Depart on the half–hour and last 1 hour and 20 minutes.
Fees:	Adults $6, children 6–12 $2. A combination ticket to the Edison and Ford homes is also available, Adults $8, children $3.
Phone:	(813) 334–3614

The Henry Ford Winter Home, Mangoes, is next door to the Edison home and features 1920s period furnishings. Henry Ford spent many winters here and often worked alongside Mr. Edison in the Edison Laboratory. Tours of the three–acre estate provide an interesting overview of the life of the inventor of the automobile and his times. The tours last approximately 45 minutes.

Location:	2350 McGregor Boulevard
Hours:	Monday through Saturday 9–4, Sunday 12:30–4, closed Thanksgiving and Christmas
Fees:	Adults $4, children 6–12 $2. A combination ticket to the Ford and Edison homes is also available, Adults $8, children $3.
Phone:	(813) 334–3614

The newest exhibit at the *Fort Myers Historical Museum* traces Southwestern Florida's agricultural history and includes a replica of a Florida Cracker's house.

Location:	2300 Peck Street
Hours:	Monday through Friday 9–4:30, Sunday 1–5, closed holidays
Fees:	Adult $2, children 2–11 50¢
Phone:	(813) 332–5955

For a fun day with the kids, plan a visit to the *Nature Center of Lee County & Planetarium.* Visit the *Audubon Aviary*, a sugar press, and an outdoor bobcat exhibit. The *Animal Olympics* and the live snake exhibit are popular with children!

Location:	3450 Ortiz Avenue
Hours:	**Nature Center: Monday** through Saturday 9–4, Sunday 11–4:30. **Planetarium**: Thursday, Friday, and Saturday at 2 and 3:15, Sunday at 2. **Laser Show**: Friday and Saturday nights at 9, 10:30, and midnight
Fees:	**Nature Center**: Adults $2, children 3–12 50¢. **Planetarium**: Adults $3, children $2. **Laser Show**: General Admission $4.50
Phone:	(813) 275–3435

Sanibel

Sanibel's shelling beaches consistently rank among the best in the world. If you search for shells, be prepared to go home with a back condition known as *The Sanibel Stoop*. To increase your knowledge and the quality of your selections, pick up a guide to Florida shells. Plan to search after storms, at and after high tide, and early in the morning.

The *J.N. "Ding" Darling National Wildlife Refuge* was established in 1945 to commemorate one of Florida's early and important environmentalists.

The natural place to begin a visit to this exceptional facility is at the Visitor's Center. If a tour is scheduled, join it. Otherwise, travel slowly along the five–mile auto tour through the mangrove forest and along the waterways. You may want to bring binoculars along.

Roseate Spoonbills

Watch for the brilliantly colored roseate spoonbills and woodstorks which have made this beautiful refuge their home. It is also recommended that you make time for the nature trail walkway or just paddle along the winding canoe trails. It is a beautiful spot to watch for birds, wildlife, and natural beauty.

Location:	One Wildlife Drive
Hours:	**Refuge**: Daily sunrise–sunset. **Visitor Center**: Early November through mid–April: Daily 9–5; Mid–April through early November: Monday through Saturday 9–4. Closed major holidays
Fees:	$3 per car and its riders, $1 for bicyclists or hikers
Phone:	(813) 472–1100

Captiva Island

Although the island's name was widely attributed to Gasparilla's habit of holding beautiful women captive on the island, the truth is far less fanciful since the name was listed on maps long before he arrived in the area. For many years, the island housed the country's largest Key Lime plantation and one of the early buildings is part of the elegant *South Seas Plantation*.

It seems important to me to relax, remove my watch, and let island time—the natural rhythm of tides and storms, sunrises and sunsets—take over. Many years ago, Anne Morrow Lindbergh visited and, as a result of that visit, was inspired to write *A Gift from the Sea*.

Be willing to share Captiva with some nocturnal residents. Raccoons are probably foraging somewhere on the island as this is being written.

Raccoons, Island Residents

Estero

The remains of an unusual pioneer settlement are preserved on the banks of the Estero River. In 1894, a religious visionary, Cyrus Reed Teed, brought his followers from Chicago to begin a New Jerusalem. His community, *Koreshan Unity*, was a celibate religious cooperative. Its growth depended on attracting new recruits. They were required to permanently turn over all their worldly possessions to the community—whether or not they stayed. Besides believing in celibacy and communal property, followers also believed the earth was a hollow sphere with all life, planets, moon, and stars within it.

Cyrus Teed expected the community would grow to 10 million people practicing the religion known as *Korenshanity*. He died in 1908 and membership declined. By 1961, the four remaining members deeded the land to the State of Florida. Twelve of the original frame buildings are on the property and several have been restored. There are nature trails along the banks of the Estero river and canoe rentals to add to your enjoyment of this interesting site.

Location:	Corner of US 41 at Corkscrew Road
Hours:	**Park:** 8–sunset. **Self–guided walks:** Daily 8–5 Ranger guided tours are available on a seasonal basis, call for details
Fees:	**Park:** $3.25 per car, with up to 8 people per vehicle **Tours:** Adults $1, children 6–13 50¢
Phone:	(813) 992–0311

Naples

Established by a Confederate veteran in the post–Civil War years, the community is well worth exploring by bicycle or on foot.

If you want to see a Deusenberg or other classic cars, plan a stop at the *Collier Automotive Museum.*

Location:	2500 Horseshoe Drive
Hours:	Wednesday through Sunday 10–6
Fees:	Adults $6, children under 13 $3
Phone:	(813) 643–5252

The *Collier County Museum's* exhibit shows the history of the county from pre–historic times to the present. The five–acre historical park also includes a recreated Seminole Village, an archaeology lab, a swamp buggy, a home from the 1920s, and a steam locomotive.

Location:	3301 Tamiami Trail East in the County Government Center
Hours:	Monday through Friday 9–5, closed holidays
Fees:	No charge
Phone:	(813) 657–3771

The *Naples Depot Civic and Cultural Center* is housed in a beautiful railroad depot. It was built for the Atlantic Coastline Railroad in 1927 and was restored in 1979.

Location:	1051 Fifth Avenue South
Hours:	Monday through Friday 10–4
Fees:	No charge
Phone:	(813) 262–1776

One word of caution: if you are planning to travel to the East Coast we do not recommend taking either the Tamiami Trail or Alligator Alley. Both these routes are desolate. We would suggest, instead, that you head North on I–75 and cross the State on Highway 27.

Beachside Walk, April 5, 1924

Cedar Key ●

Homosassa Springs ●

Brooksville ●
Masaryktown ●
Tarpon Springs ●
Indian Shores ●
Clearwater ● ● TAMPA
Largo ●

The farther North you travel on this tour, the more the area begins to resemble the Florida of the early 20th century. Travel to some of the state's oldest sponge beds and then through hardwood forests to Cedar Key, once the other end of the rail line that began on Amelia Island. Cedar Key, with its bayous, turn–of–the–century dwellings, and uneasy truce with hurricanes, provides a look at the survival of a naturally beautiful Florida.

Clearwater

Henry Plant was the West Coast's railroading entrepreneur. He believed in Clearwater and established a railroad station and a major tourist resort here.

His hotel, the ***Belleview Biltmore Hotel***, opened in 1897. It is interesting to walk through this classic turn–of–the–century building. The hotel remains the largest occupied wooden structure in the world and is on the National Register of Historic Places.

The Belleview Biltmore

141

In the 1940s, all 365 rooms were used by the U.S. Air Force as a barracks. The building has been restored and today's guided tour through the restored Victorian hotel features antiques and Queen Anne decor.

Location:	25 Belleview Boulevard
Hours:	Tours: Monday through Saturday at 11 am
Fees:	Adults $5, children $3
Phone:	(813) 442–6171

The Clearwater Marine Science Center, Aquarium, and Museum has live and model displays of area marine life. Be sure to see the sea turtle and dolphin tanks. The facility is committed to the rescue, treatment, and release of marine mammals and sea turtles. It is particularly important to note that it is one of only eight in the nation with similar marine mammal and sea turtle responsibilities.

Location:	249 Windward Passage
Hours:	Monday through Friday 9–5, Saturday and Sunday 11–4, closed holidays
Fees:	Adults $2.75, children 3–11 $1.50
Phone:	(813) 441–1790 or (813) 447–0980

If you're ready for a change of scene and an outdoor adventure, visit *Moccasin Lake Nature Center*. The nature trails are just about perfect for an afternoon hike and the interpretive center provides interesting background on the setting and the wildlife you may see.

Location:	2750 Park Trail Lane
Hours:	Tuesday through Friday 9–5, Saturday and Sunday 10–6, closed July 4, Thanksgiving, the day after Christmas and New Year's Day
Fees:	Adults $1, children 3–12, 50¢
Phone:	(813) 462–6024

Largo

There is an excellent photography collection showing the lives of the area's pioneers at the *Pinellas County Historical Museum.* While thinking about the pioneers, walk through the adjacent *Heritage Park*. Over a dozen historically significant buildings have been assembled to reconstruct the area's setting as it might have been.

Location:	11909 125th Street North
Hours:	Tuesday through Saturday 10–4, Sunday 1–4. Tours throughout the day, with the last one starting at 3:30, closed national holidays
Fees:	No charge, donations welcome
Phone:	(813) 462–3474

Indian Shores

Suncoast Seabird Sanctuary is a refuge and rehabilitation center for injured wild birds. Opened in the early 1970s, the Sanctuary now cares for up to 500 birds at a time.

Location:	18328 Gulf Boulevard
Hours:	Daily 9–sunset. Guided tours at 2 on Tuesdays and the first Sunday of the month
Fees:	No charge, donations welcome
Phone:	(813) 391–6211

Tarpon Springs

The town was founded in 1876 and named in the mistaken belief that tarpon spawned in the nearby Spring Bayou. Shortly thereafter, a small group of Greek fishermen settled in the area to harvest sponge. They worked near shore and used the old country techniques of hooking sponges with long poles in shallow water.

In the early 20th century, deep sea diving equipment was developed. Although there was a lot of trial and error, the advances were watched with interest and were largely successful. The Tarpon Springs sponge divers began using deep sea diving equipment in 1905. Wearing copper–helmeted diving suits, they were able to work far out to sea harvesting the rich sponge beds.

As the equipment was perfected, so was Tarpon Springs' hold on the industry. Synthetic sponges had not been invented and it became a multimillion dollar business. Pardon the pun, but the tide turned by mid–century due to a red tide disease which harmed the sponge beds and the introduction and rapid acceptance of synthetic sponges.

*Tarpon Springs
Fisherman
Threading Sponges,
May 1944*

Although most of the divers' finds have been sponges, occasionally they bring other treasures to the surface.

In 1938, a local sponge diver, Sozon Vatikiosis, brought in two seashells of previously unknown varieties. They were sent to the Smithsonian Institution and were later described as tea–rose blossoms which had turned to stone. The shells were named in honor of the diver and his wife and became part of the Smithsonian's permanent collection. It is interesting to wonder under what conditions and where these beautiful roses had bloomed, and when and how they were turned into such exquisite seashells.

St. Nicholas Greek Orthodox Cathedral is a fine example of neo–Byzantine architecture. The icons, stained glass, and Grecian marble are particularly beautiful in the Cathedral, built in 1943.

Location:	30 North Pinellas Avenue
Hours:	Daily
Fees:	Donations accepted
Phone:	(813) 937–3540

Learn about the sponge diving process at the *Spongeorama Exhibit Center* and *Museum of Sponge Diving.* While here, be sure to see the 15–minute film on the sponge diving process and tour the working sponge factory.

Location:	510 Dodecanes Boulevard
Hours:	Daily 10–6
Fees:	**Museum**: no charge. **Theater**: Adults $1.50, children 4–12, 75¢
Phone:	(813) 942–3771

Masaryktown

Masaryktown was named for the first President of Czechoslovakia. It was founded in 1924 by Joseph Joscak, editor of a Czech newspaper in New York City. For many years it was culturally isolated and many of the original settlers spoke only Czech. The area still has a large Czech population and visitors are welcomed to the community's cultural festival.

Brooksville

Look around the center of town. In the 1870s, there were no paved roads. The superhighway of its day was known as a Corduroy Road. It was made by paving trails with logs so the stages could travel over the mud. One of these "superhighways" was the route used by the stagecoach which raced through Brooksville on the way between Gainesville and Tampa.

Homosassa Springs

Homosassa Springs Wildlife Park features a floating observatory where visitors can go below water level to view thousands of freshwater fish, saltwater fish, and manatees—Florida's endangered marine mammals. It is one of the few places in the world where manatees may be observed at close range throughout the year. Enjoy the excellent manatee interpretive programs and a scenic boat trip up Pepper Creek.

Location:	9225 West Fishbowl Drive (1/4 mile West of US 19, turn at light and follow signs)
Hours:	Daily 9–5:30
Fees:	Adults $6.95, children 3–12 $3.95
Phone:	(904) 628–2311

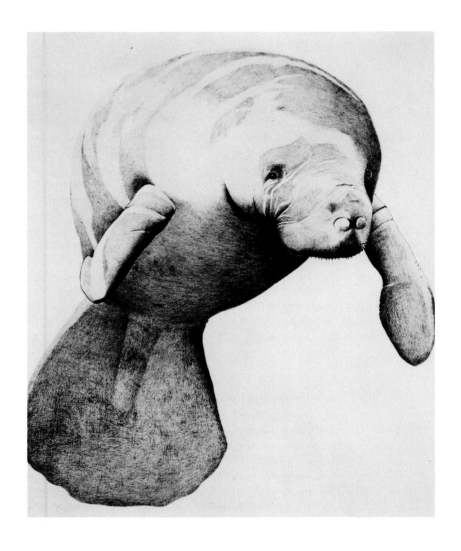

The Gentle Manatee
An Endangered Species

Cedar Key

The area was settled in the early 1840s and it became a thriving port city. At first, goods were shipped by water. Then, with the development of the cross–state railroad, cotton, lumber, and naval stores travelled by rail to Amelia Island and then North and East.

Unfortunately, the boom did not last. During the Civil War, blockade runners brought food and war materials for the Confederacy to Cedar Key's port. Salt, needed by the Southern armies, was made locally by boiling and evaporating sea water in large iron basins. The Federalists were aware of these activities and, in 1862, a Union force attacked by sea, captured Cedar Key, and brought a halt to its then war–based economy.

After the war, the townspeople turned to timber. Pine and cypress were cut and shipped, cedar was and still is used to manufacture pencils. As the natural timber reserves were depleted in the 1880s, the area's residents turned to commercial fishing— which is still done on a small scale. However, today's Cedar Key has an uneasy economy which is largely dependent on fishing and tourism.

The *Cedar Key Historical Society Museum* shows the town's history through photographs dating back to the early 1800s.

Location:	Route 24 at 2nd Street
Hours:	Monday through Saturday 10–5, Sunday 1–5
Fees:	Adults $1, children 6–12 50¢

The visitor center at the *Cedar Key State Museum* contains exhibits which depict the colorful history of the area.

Location:	Museum Drive, 1–3/4 miles North of Route 24
Hours:	Thursday through Monday 9–5
Fees:	Adults 50¢
Phone:	(904) 543–5350

Gulf
Coast
Florida

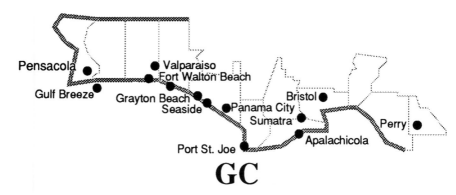

GC

The Florida Panhandle covers a vast area of land. As you will note, the Gulf Coast portion of the Panhandle has historic cities, woods, wetlands, refuges, and magnificent beaches.

Throughout Florida's early constitutional history, various political and economic factions held strong views regarding how involved Florida should be with the United States. In Tour 16, the *Start of Statehood,* you travel to the site where all of the differences were resolved—at least for a short time.

Florida has many riches, among them a vast variety of beaches. Most long–time residents have a favorite beach and would be happy if no one else ever found it. Thus, a dilemma develops when it comes to talking about beaches. Whatever your personal choice, spend some time at the *Extraordinary Beaches* described in Tour 17.

Pensacola's location at the mouth of a deep water harbor has made it an important stronghold from the start of European exploration in the area. The city is highlighted in Tour 18.

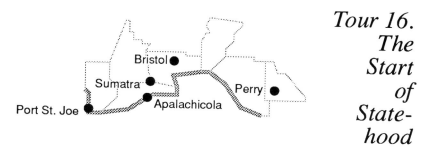

Tour 16. The Start of State-hood

The area through which you drive combines vast stretches of timberland with several of Florida's important early communities. You will see a town which became a ghost town—and was then repopulated. You'll also see a replica of the first air conditioner invented and the site where Florida's first constitution was drafted.

Perry

The importance of forestry in Florida dates back to the early 1800s. The *Forest Capital State Museum* commemorates the longleaf pine that built so many of Florida's early homes and businesses. Also on the property is the *North Florida Cracker Homestead Interpretive Site*. The homestead is typical of cabins that dotted the pinewoods of North Florida at the start of the 20th century.

Location: 204 Forest Park Drive, South of Perry on US 19
Hours: Thursday through Monday 9–12 and 1–5, closed
              Thanksgiving, Christmas, and New Year's Day
Fees: Adults 50¢
Phone: (904) 584–3227

Route 98 West travels through forest and wildlife refuges before curving away from the coast onto Route 65 North. Follow 65 North to see Sumatra and Bristol before returning to Route 98 West and the Coastal route.

Sumatra

During the War of 1812, the *Fort Gadsden State Historic Site* was used for recruiting and training Blacks and Indians. Its location served as a threat to supply vessels headed to the U.S.

territorial boundary, 50 miles North. The British ordered the Fort's destruction.

The battle which followed was one of the shortest in naval history. The fifth shot from the gunboats landed in the Fort's magazine killing 90% of the 300 men, women, and children then living there. A miniature replica of the original outpost and six historic exhibits are on display.

Location:	6 miles Southwest of Sumatra, off Route 65
Hours:	Daily 8–sunset
Fees:	No charge
Phone:	(904) 670–8988

Bristol

Some biblical historians say that Noah's Ark was built in *Torreya State Park*. They say that the Ark was built from lumber from the Torreya tree, which only grows in four locations in the world—Bristol, Northern California, Japan, and China.

The scholars also note the location of the nearby rivers as being referenced in the Bible.

Whether or not these issues can ever be resolved, Torreya State Park is still an interesting place for seeing the unusual tree, taking a walk, and having a picnic. Walk to the steep riverside bluffs that rise more than 150 feet above the water and note hardwood trees that are rarely seen South of Northern Georgia.

While visiting, be sure to see the *Gregory House*. It was built in 1849 and moved to the park in 1935. Tours are conducted through the house which is furnished to reflect the life styles of the 1800s.

Location:	Route 2, 13 miles Northwest of Bristol
Hours:	**Park**: Daily 8–sundown. **Tours** at 10, 2, and 4
Fees:	**Park**: $2 per vehicle. **Tours**: Adults $1, children over 13 50¢
Phone:	(904) 643–2674

Apalachicola

For 10,000 years, the Apalachee Indians occupied this land. Called the "land beyond the river," at least nine Spanish missions had been built in the area by 1665.

William Augustus Bowles, an Englishmen, reached this section of the Gulf of Mexico in the 18th century. He was an adventurer and pirate.

William Augustus Bowles

Legend suggests that he came to Florida at the age of 12, married the daughter of a Creek Indian Chief, and terrorized the Spaniards while trying to break their hold on East and West Florida. A somewhat different legend says that he was dismissed from the British Navy, moved to Georgia, married the Creek Indian woman, and became influential in tribal matters.

In any event, he led a band of Creek against the Spanish in the Siege of Pensacola in 1781 and was taken prisoner by the Spaniards who imprisoned him in Madrid. In 1799, he escaped and rejoined the Creek tribe near Apalachicola Bay. The Bay area became his headquarters and he looted surrounding towns and preyed on ships at sea. He was again taken prisoner and died in 1805 thus ending a frightening part of Apalachicola's history.

As cotton became an important agricultural crop in the Panhandle, the Apalachicola harbor became famous and the town prospered. However, as railroading matured, it signalled doom for the harbor area. By 1916, oysters began to be cultivated as a cash crop. The area now has more than 180,000 acres of oyster beds and the sweet, delicious Apalachicola oyster is known throughout the world.

Oysters—Big Business in Apalachicola

You probably arrived in Apalachicola in an air conditioned car—and may have slept in an air conditioned hotel last night.

Try to imagine yourself in Apalachicola in 1845. Air conditioning had not been invented. A terrible yellow fever epidemic was spreading from house to house. The town's doctor, *John Gorrie,* was trying to ease his patients' suffering. In trying to make them more comfortable, he thought of cooling the air. And so, he invented the first ice–making machine to provide air cooled relief for his patients.

Although Dr. Gorrie patented the invention in 1851, he had little cash, was ridiculed in the national press, and was unable to capitalize on the invention. He died in 1855 without having gained recognition for his work. Since that time, his original air conditioning machine has been placed on display in the Smithsonian Institution and a replica is part of the exhibit at this museum.

Location:	6th Street at Avenue D
Hours:	Thursday through Monday 9–12 and 1–5. Closed Thanksgiving, Christmas and New Year's Day
Fees:	Adults and children over 6 50¢
Phone:	(904) 653–9347

Port St. Joe

Although today's community is a growing timber and papermaking center with wide streets and lovely homes, it was not always so. In 1835, the village occupying the site was known as St. Joseph. It was a boom town competing with Apalachicola for the cotton and river trade.

Eighty–six territorial delegates met in 1838 at the site of today's *Constitution Convention State Museum*. Their task was to draft Florida's first constitution. St. Joseph became the meeting place only because it represented a neutral site between the political antagonists in Eastern/Western and Middle Florida.

Florida had been an American territory since 1821. Many Floridians, especially those living in the prosperous mid–section, had long favored a change from territory to statehood. However, the powerful Eastern and Western Florida factions opposed state-hood. Their argument was that Florida was too poor to assume the financial burdens statehood would impose.

The first of Florida's five constitutions was drafted by the convention that met on December 3, 1838. The political figures completed the framework for Florida's future on January 11, 1861. On the same day the convention voted to submit the completed constitution to the people of the state for ratification, they also submitted paperwork to the U.S. Congress as the formal application of the people of Florida for admission to the Union. Talk about forgetting due process—and its repercussions!

For the next six years, the people of Florida spoke again and again. The beleaguered Legislative Council petitioned Congress for immediate admission to the Union, then for indefinite postponement, and then for division into two territories. Congress finally passed an act admitting Florida into the Union on March 3, 1845.

As an important footnote, it should be noted that the state seceded from the Union in 1861 and rejoined the United States in 1865 after the Civil War.

Location:	200 Allen Memorial Way
Hours:	Thursday through Monday 9–12 and 1–5, closed Thanksgiving, Christmas and New Year's Day
Fees:	Adults 50¢
Phone:	(904) 229–8029

It was mentioned that the town became a ghost town. During the boom it had grown to 12,000 inhabitants. In a short period of time, the residents felt the economic reversals, and were struck by a major yellow fever epidemic and a hurricane. The survivors fled. Most of the abandoned houses and businesses were dismantled and moved by boat to Apalachicola. By 1846, all that remained of the village was the cemetery.

The name change and later growth and settlement have been largely due to the paper and pulp industry.

Tour 17.

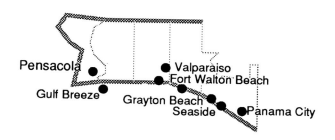

Extraordinary Beaches

By now, it is expected that the traveller anticipates surprises along the tour. Major military installations, past and present, provide a constant reminder of the area's importance in protecting the coastline and shipping lanes. Beachfront honky–tonk gives way to one of the country's most beautiful beaches near a modern–day rendition of a Florida seaside resort. Throughout the area, the tour combines Gulf Coast scenery with heavily wooded stretches.

Panama City

Spanish explorers landed here in the first half of the 16th century, English settlement began about a hundred years later, and American pioneers followed. *The Junior Museum of Bay County* tells the story of how the early pioneers lived, logged, and farmed.

Location:	1731 Jenks Avenue
Hours:	**Labor Day to Memorial Day**: Tuesday through Friday 9–4:30, Saturday 10–4, closed holidays **Summer**: Monday through Friday 9–4:30
Fees:	No charge
Phone:	(904) 769–6128

Panama City Beach

The powdery, white sand beaches along this portion of the coast originated thousands of years ago as quartz crystals in the

155

Appalachian Mountains. Over time, these crystals were sifted, washed, ground, polished, and slowly pushed South to be deposited along the beachfront.

Offshore, the *Yucatan Current* (part of the Gulf Stream) draws dolphin, marlin, sailfish, tuna, and other fish to the area. It is a fisherman's paradise. *City Pier* extends 1,600 feet into the Gulf of Mexico. Put a fishing line into the water. You very well may reel in tonight's dinner.

Grayton Beach

Many Floridians have their favorite beach. This is mine.

Another Perfect Florida Beach...

Seaside

Seaside is an architectural gem which has won international acclaim. The beachside resort area offers Victorian pitched roofs, white picket fences, and small–town civilities. Park in the shopping area, browse through the public spaces, and look carefully at the architecture and site usage. The beach pavilions, which are all different, combine various kinds of lattice work and serve to frame a picture–perfect stretch of sand and sea. An architecture stop or a weekend visit is highly recommended.

Location:	Route 30A
Phone:	(800) 635–0296 or (904) 231–4224

Destin

The *De Soto Canyon* is located about 30 miles offshore and is a favorite spot for sailfishing. The small *Museum of the Sea and Indian* shows animals and shells in preserved form, as well as American Indian artifacts from most of the United States and South America.

Location:	4801 Beach Highway (Highway 98 East)
Hours:	Memorial Day to Labor Day 8–7, Labor Day to Memorial Day 8–4
Fees:	Adults $3.75, seniors $3.45, children 5–16 $2
Phone:	(904) 837–6625

Fort Walton Beach

The area was once an important Indian settlement and meeting place. The *Indian Temple Mound Museum* tells the story of the Fort Walton Indian Culture's village which housed 1,000–2,000 people. In today's terminology, the settlement served as the "county seat" for the area's Indians. A large collection of pottery has been found which dates back 3,500 years. Exhibits in the museum show 10,000 years of Gulf Coast living by the Southern Indians. Be careful when parking and entering the museum. A busy highway is just beyond the mounds. The preservation of the Florida Indian culture is a continuing challenge as the area grows.

Location:	139 Miraclestrip Parkway
Hours:	September through May: Monday through Friday 12–4, Saturday 9–4. Balance of year: Monday through Saturday 9–4, Sunday 12:30–4
Fees:	Adults and children over 12 75¢
Phone:	(904) 243–6521

Valpariso

During World War II, a heroic group of pilots trained at *Eglin Air Force Base* for special duty with General James Doolittle. A good place to start learning about the Air Force is the *U.S. Air Force Armament Museum.*

Come see the formerly top secret SR–71 Blackbird reconnaissance plane. It was so secret that its existence was denied for over 20 years. The Museum displays over 5,000 items, including the enormous F–105 Thunderchief (Vietnam era), the supersonic F–104 Starfighter, and a B–29 bomber. A 32–minute film, *Arming the Air Force*, screens continuously and tells the history of Eglin Air Force Base and its role in the development of armament.

Location:	6 miles North of US 98 on Route 85, on Eglin Air Force Base property
Hours:	Daily 9:30–4:30, closed Thanksgiving, Christmas, and New Year's Day
Fees:	No charge
Phone:	(904) 651–1808

Gulf Breeze

Florida became a territory in 1821. Development of a fortification system along the coast began soon after. In both Florida and Mississippi, these forts are now part of the *Gulf Islands National Seashore* which also includes an 150–mile strip of barrier islands, natural harbors, and submerged lands.

Fort Pickens was built by the U.S. Corps of Engineers between 1829 and 1834 to assist in the defense of Pensacola Bay and the Naval Shipyard. Between 1886 and 1890 it was the prison for Geronimo, the Apache chief and medicine man. The fort is a good place for exploring and also to see the nature exhibits, the marine life aquariums, and to take a waterside tour.

Location: 1400 Fort Pickens Road
Hours: April through October: Daily 9–5, November
                  through March: Daily 9–4
Fees: $3 per person
Phone: (904) 932–5307

Florida's signature tree is the live oak. Its interesting history is shown at the *Naval Live Oaks Park*. The live oak has evergreen leaves, a leathery trunk, crooked branches, and can grow to 40–50 feet in height. It is often covered with Spanish moss and provides the shading canopies for so many of the older roads in the state.

Florida Live Oaks

In addition to its beauty, live oak timber has been important to the U.S. for over 200 years.

The heaviest of all oak timber, it is resistant to disease and decay. Live oak timber from this area was used to build the USS Constitution in the 1790s. When the vessel was in action against the British during the War of 1812, it was nicknamed *Old Ironsides* because of the strength of its timber and its fine construction. Over 150 years later, repairs were needed. They were done in this area and, of course, again used live oak timber.

Stop at the Visitors Center to learn more about the trees before you begin to tour this interesting site.

Location:	1801 Gulf Breeze Parkway
Hours:	Daily 8:30–5
Fees:	No charge
Phone:	(904) 934–2600

Colossus, a lowland gorilla, is always a popular attraction at the *Zoo*. There are also Bengal tigers and alligators. Hop aboard the Safari Line Train for a bird's–eye view of the animals, botanical gardens, and natural landscapes.

Location:	5701 Gulf Breeze Parkway
Hours:	Daily 9–5. Closed Thanksgiving and Christmas
Fees:	Adults $7.50, seniors (over 55) $6.50, children 3–11 $4.50
Phone:	(904) 932–2229

Tour 18.
Pensacola, City of Five Flags

Pensacola has one of the most colorful histories of any city in Florida. Although St. Augustine is recognized as the oldest, continuous European settlement in the country, it should be noted that the *first* settlement was in Pensacola. The distinction is important here.

Spanish settlers arrived in Pensacola harbor in 1559. They stayed for two years before being driven away by hurricanes and Indian attacks. During the next 300 years, many other colonists wanted control of the harbor. At various times, Pensacola's citizens have lived under five flags. Indeed, the community changed hands 17 times among the five captor nations. Finally, in 1752, King Ferdinand VI managed to take and keep control.

In the pre–Civil War period, Pensacola operated as a stockade, a frontier outpost, and a rollicking port city. Following the war, the timber industry prospered as the pine and cypress forests were harvested. No one seemed to consider how the community would support itself when their easy access to wood ran out. That occurred just as Pensacola became a military town.

Pensacola Harbor, early etching

The area's economy stabilized again with the establishment of the U.S. Naval Air Station in 1914.

A good place to begin a visit to Pensacola is walking through the *Historic Pensacola Village*. It presents seven restorations of colonial Pensacola buildings dating from 1803. The complex provides a chance to look at West Florida's history through the *Museum of Commerce, the Museum of Industry, the Julee Cottage Museum of Black History, the Dorr, Lavalle and Quina House Museums* and several others. Within this small district, it is possible to see examples of how early Pensacolans lived as well as beautiful examples of Spanish, French Creole, and Greek Revival architecture.

Location:	205 East Zaragoza Street
Fees:	One ticket admits guests to both the Village and the Wentworth Museum. Adults $4, seniors (over 65) and military personnel $3, children 4–16 $2
Hours:	Monday through Saturday 10–4:30, Sunday 1–4:30, closed Christmas and New Year's Day
Phone:	(904) 444–8905

In its earlier days, Pensacolans built grand buildings. The *T. T. Wentworth, Jr. Florida State Museum* is housed in what used to be Pensacola's city hall, a large Renaissance Revival style building built in 1907–08. On the third floor of this imposing structure is a hands–on museum for children.

Location:	320 Jefferson Street
Fees:	One ticket admits guests to both the Village and the Wentworth Museum. Adults $4, seniors (over 65) and military personnel $3, children 4–16 $2
Hours:	Monday through Saturday 10–4:30, Sunday 1–4:30, closed Christmas and New Year's Day
Phone:	(904) 444–8586

When you're ready to walk into the 20th century, drive over to the *North Hill Preservation District*. This area contains over 500 homes, many of which were built in the city's lumbering era. It is one of the loveliest upper middle class residential and historic districts in the state. A good place to begin a walk is at the corner of Blunt and Spring Streets.

If you've never had the opportunity to practice a boarding house reach, plan to eat at the *Hopkins Boarding House*.

Location	900 North Spring Street in the North Hill Preservation District
Hours:	No meals served Sunday evenings and Monday. Otherwise, breakfast from 7–9:30, lunch 11:15–2, dinner 5:15–7:30
Fees:	Moderate fees, homemade, homestyle, ample meals
Phone:	(904) 438–3979

The *Pensacola Historical Museum* is housed in *Old Christ Church*, the oldest church building in Florida that is still in its original location. The exhibits show the development of Pensacola from the Indian era to the early 1900s and provide a good counterpoint to the Pensacola Village environment.

Location:	405 South Adams Street
Hours:	Monday through Saturday 9–4:30, closed holidays
Fees:	Adults $2, children $1
Phone:	(904) 433–1559

Pensacola's oldest settlement began in what is now the *Seville Historic District*. The area has been particularly important since the late 1700s and now has a rare concentration of Creole, Victorian, and other styles of homes dating from the 1780s to the late 1800s.

Location:	Area surrounding 130 East Government Street

The first naval air station in the country began here in 1914 and the Pensacola *Naval Air Station* remains one of the country's major facilities.

Blue Angels, ca. 1962

Try to arrange your visit when a Winging Ceremony is taking place. It often concludes with a *Blue Angels Airshow*.

The *National Museum of Naval Aviation* contains outstanding examples of Navy, Marine Corps, and Coast Guard aircraft from the past 80 years. There are over 100 aircraft, an exact replica of an Apollo Space Suit, and almost 100 scale models of aircraft, dirigibles, and spacecraft. Of particular interest are the F–4 and A–7 jet cockpit simulators. Strap yourself in and take the controls!

You'll appreciate its size when you're touring, but be aware that the National Museum of Naval Aviation is one of the three largest air and space museums in the world. If it is man–made and flies, look for it here first!

Location:	3465 Taylor Road, on the Naval Air Station Grounds
Hours:	Daily 9–5, closed Thanksgiving, Christmas, and New Year's Day
Fees:	No charge
Phone:	(904) 452–3604

Two forts were built in the early 19th century to protect the emerging Pensacola Navy Yard. *Fort Barrancas* was built between 1839–1844 and the *Advanced Redoubt* was built a little later. It was only manned by soldiers during the Civil War. Be sure to stop at the Information Center before walking through the Fort.

Location:	On the Naval Air Station Grounds
Hours:	Daily 9–5
Fees:	No charge

For information about all activities at the *Naval Air Station* which are open to the public, telephone (904) 433–1559.

The
Northern
Panhandle

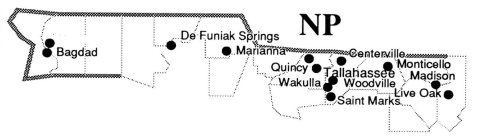

The Northern Panhandle is the most Southern part of Florida you will visit. Four tours are highlighted in this section.

In Tour 19, we travel along *The Spanish Explorers Trail* to find springs and towns which are relatively untouched by the 20th century.

Tallahassee, The Capitol Connection leads to the two capitol buildings in the heart of the city. After taking a good look at government in action, make time for museums, universities, scenery, and history. They are all part of Tour 20.

Indian myths and pioneers populate Tour 21 as you explore *Canopy Roads and Indian Springs.*

The last tour in this section, *The Tobacco Road*, returns to the days of plantations and tobacco auctions as you continue to put today's Florida into perspective.

Tour 19.
The
Spanish
Explorers
Trail

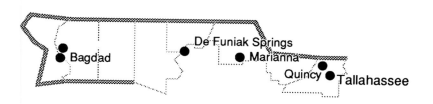

Many Spanish explorers traveled North from Pensacola along old Indian trails. They mapped the trails and the route then became known as the Old Spanish Trail. Although Ponce de León was one of the most famous 16th century explorers to travel this way, realize that many Indians, explorers, settlers, and modern day transportation specialists have all had a part in developing this route. Highlights of the trip include seeing part of the antebellum South and noting agricultural communities which once made this region prosperous.

Bagdad

What imagination someone had as they were naming the town—and what a wonderful name to find in lumbering country!

As had been the case with Pensacola, Bagdad's lumbering economy flourished from around 1820 to 1930. Today, its economic prosperity has passed, leaving behind a quiet village with dozens of restored Victorian houses.

Milton

Once Milton was a thriving outpost of sawmills, lumbermen, and townspeople. Four–masted schooners and shipping steamers landed at its piers. Today's community is much more quiet. The **Milton Opera House and Imogene Theatre** in the center of town have been restored and remind us of the city's early cultural legacy.

A quick trip into the 20th century awaits you with a visit to **Whiting Field**, the busiest military airport in the Southeast and the third busiest military airport in the world. It is the center for the military's T–34 fixed wing aircraft and TH–57 helicopter training. Tours are available with advance reservation and are quite interesting—particularly if you've always wanted to crawl into a T–34 and experience flight simulation.

Location:	8 miles North on I–90
Hours:	Monday through Friday 7:30–2
Fees:	No charge
Phone:	(904) 623–7651

DeFuniak Springs

In the early 20th century, this small town became one of Florida's leading intellectual centers. It was the site of a winter Chautauqua camp. Turn off the highway and take a pleasant drive around the almost circular spring–fed lake. While driving, note the white Chautauqua buildings on the Western side of the lake and stop at the small library.

An Early Chautauqua Program Looks Familiar

167

For a totally unexpected treat, step into the library to see an amazing collection of armor—some of which dates back to the Crusades.

Marianna

Founded in 1829, Marianna was named for the daughters of a pioneer merchant. The town grew because of its location as a covered wagon crossing point and as one of the stops on the stage coach route.

Early Immigrants,
the Wagon Train Arrivals, ca. 1875

Stop at the *Florida Caverns State Park* to cool off on a hot day. There are wonderful local legends about the caverns ranging from how people were hidden in them to how some of the important townspeople came and went between the caverns and city buildings. Today's visit to the caves is a cool treat. Be sure to bring a sweater with you to wear once you go underground.

Location:	3 miles North on Route 167
Hours:	**Park:** Daily 8–sunset. **Cavern tours:** daily 9–4
Fees:	**Cavern:** Adults $3, children 3–12 $1.50
Phone:	(904) 482–9598

Quincy

Settled around 1824, Quincy attracted wealthy planters and politicians from farther North. There was a great deal of sentiment against the Union forces throughout the Panhandle's Northern tier. Quincy's citizens were among the most belligerent anti–Unionists in the State. A few years before Florida seceded from the Republic, Quincy Guards seized arms and ammunition from a U.S. Arsenal on the Apalachicola River.

In 1893, a deposit of fuller's earth was discovered in the area. The clay was discovered along the river banks and has been open–pit mined in a 25–mile radius of the town. By the 1930s, the area produced more than half the fuller's earth used in the U.S.

The land, natural resources, and quick thinking helped Quincy residents became millionaires. For example, early in the 20th century, a Quincy banker heard about Coca–Cola from friends in Georgia. He told many townspeople and they invested wisely, fortunes were made.

As you stroll through the community, note the old fashioned gardens of jasmine, camellias, and roses as well as the beautiful Queen Anne and Greek Revival homes in the Historic District.

Robert Stephens with the first load of Coca–Cola bottled in Quincy, 1908

Tallahassee, a City with Two Capitols

Tour 20.
Tallahassee,
The
Capitol
Connection

Tallahassee

Tallahassee is Florida's capitol city and owes that honor to its location. At the time of statehood, peninsular Florida had not been widely settled and had not emerged as a political force. The state's major political figures were from Pensacola and Jacksonville. These factions rarely agreed on anything and were competitive in almost everything. It was clear that neither group would give in and let the other city be chosen as the new state capitol. Tallahassee was selected simply because it was located midway between the home cities of the political rivals.

It is rare to find a state with two capitol buildings. *The Old Capitol* has been restored to its 1902 appearance and is a good starting point to review the state's historic displays. Of particular interest is the eight room permanent exhibit, *A View from the Capitol*, which tells the story of Florida's colorful and vibrant political history.

Location: 400 South Monroe
  Street
Hours: Monday through Friday
  9–4:30, Saturday 10–4:30,
  Sunday and holidays 12–4:30,
  closed Christmas
Fees: No charge
Phone: (904) 487–1902

The Old Capitol, as seen from the Vietnam War Veterans' Memorial.

The State's legislation is enacted in *The New Capitol* . Call ahead to check the legislative schedule and then plan to watch government in action. If no sessions are underway, go to the 22nd floor observatory for a panoramic view of the city. This building, opened in 1977, was one of the last designed by Edward Durrell Stone.

Location:	South Adams Street
Hours:	Monday through Friday 8–5. **Guided tours**: Monday through Friday 9–4, Saturday, Sunday and holidays 11–3. Closed Easter, Labor Day, Thanksgiving, Christmas and New Year's Day
Fees:	No charge
Phone:	(904) 488–6167

Search for the sunken treasures of old Spanish galleons, examine Civil War memorabilia, and learn more about the steamboat era at the *Museum of Florida History*. This is a major state resource.

Location:	500 South Bronough Street in the R. A. Gray Building
Hours:	Monday through Friday 9–4:30, Saturday 10–4:30, Sunday and holidays 12–4:30, closed Christmas
Fees:	No charge, donations accepted
Phone:	(904) 488–1484

The largest collection of African–American documents and artifacts in the Southeast is housed at the *Black Archives Museum and Research Center.*

Location:	On the Florida A&M University campus at the corner of Martin Luther King Boulevard and Gamble Streets
Hours:	Daily 9–4
Fees:	No charge
Phone:	(904) 599–3020

Tallahassee's oldest surviving building is the *Columns*, built in the early 1800s.

Location:	100 North Duval Street
Hours:	Monday through Friday 9–5
Fees:	No charge
Phone:	(904) 224–8116

Two interesting areas for a walk or a drive are the *Calhoun Street Historical District Downtown* and the *Park Avenue Historical District Downtown*. Much of the housing stock was built in the 1830–1880 period and has been restored.

Peruvian, Japanese, and 20th century American paintings are highlights of the *Fine Arts Gallery and Museum*.

Location:	Fine Arts Building, Florida State University Campus
Hours:	**September through June:** Monday through Friday 10–4, Saturday and Sunday 1–4. **July through August:** Monday through Friday, 10–4, Sunday 1–4, closed University holidays
Fees:	No charge
Phone:	(904) 644–6836

The next portion of the tour involves short drives beyond the downtown district.

Children enjoy the *Tallahassee Jr. Museum* where they can safely see a Florida panther's habitat and a red wolf's den. While there, also be sure to see the 1850 plantation house and the 1880s farmstead.

Location:	3945 Museum Drive
Hours:	Tuesday through Saturday 9–5, Sunday 12:30–5, closed Thanksgiving, Christmas Eve, Christmas, and New Year's Day
Fees:	Adults $4, seniors (over 65) $3, children 4–15 $2
Phone:	(904) 576–1636 and (904) 575–8684

In 1923, the *Alfred B. Maclay State Gardens* property was purchased. Mr. Maclay, a New York financier, and his wife created the gardens as part of their winter retreat. Garden tours are conducted on Saturdays and Sundays during the peak blooming times in mid–March. Try to visit in December to see the camellias and between January and April to tour the house.

Location:	3540 Thomasville Road
Hours:	Daily 8–sunset
Fees:	$3.25 per vehicle, including up to 8 people
Phone:	(904) 487–4556

173

Although the *Lake Jackson Indian Mounds State Archaeological Site* is a now a quiet park, it was once one of the most important gathering places for Indians of this region. There are six earth temple mounds and one burial mound on this site. They are the remains of a ceremonial center that existed between 1200 and 1500 AD. The largest mound is 278 feet x 312 feet at the base and approximately 36 feet in height. Climb to the top and imagine being able to observe and speak with several tribes that would have been encamped in the area.

While in the park, find your way to the lake. It is said that Hernando de Soto and his 600 man army spent the winter of 1539 living in the Indian village here. It was here that he and his troops celebrated what would be recognized as the first U.S. Christmas.

Location:	Crowder Road off US 27 North
Hours:	Daily 8–sunset
Fees:	No charge
Phone:	(904) 562–0042

San Luis Archaeological and Historic Site was the location of a Spanish town (founded in 1633) and an Apalachee Indian village. The area contained an Indian council house, a Christian church, a Spanish fort, homes, and outbuildings. When Britain was invading the area in 1704, residents decided their town would not be captured and they burned it to the ground.

Visitors are welcome to watch state archaeologists at the 50–acre site as more of this important historic village is uncovered.

Take the trail walk to see exhibits that tell the story of the early inhabitants, as well as today's search for the past. Also try to make time to see the Indian and Spanish artifacts and plan to take a guided tour.

Location:	2020 Mission Road
Hours:	Monday through Friday 9–4:30, Saturday 10–4:30, Sunday 12–4:30. **Excavations:** late February through early May, tours available daily
Fees:	No charge
Phone:	(904) 487–3711 for tour information

Centerville

Wakulla Woodville

Saint Marks

Tour 21. Canopy Roads and Indian Springs

Tour 21 is for people who take their leisure seriously. If you have time before leaving Tallahassee, stop at the State Archives and search out some of the early maps. The old Canopy Roads, planted by Florida's pioneers are perfect for a leisurely afternoon outing. Bring a bathing suit and look for legendary creatures, bike the old railroad route, and just relax.

Heading North

Canopy Roads are Florida's moss–draped, live oak boundaried byways. They serve as a reminder of stage coach days and the era when early settlers came in creaking wagon trains along dirt roads seeking their new Florida homes.

The early settlers planted their roadways with live oak trees. Now secondary roads, five of the state's old canopied settlers' routes are particularly beautiful.

A Canopy Road

The old Centerville Road is featured in this tour. When you have time, also plan to find the Meridian, Miccosukee, Old Bainbridge, and St. Augustine canopy roads. They are all noted for their beauty.

When you drive the *Centerville Canopy Road*, be sure to stop at *Bradley's Country Store*. This 1927 store still makes and sells its famous homemade country sausage.

Location:	12 miles North of Tallahassee on Centerville Road
Hours:	Monday through Saturday 8–6
Phone:	(904) 893–1647

The Marquis de Lafayette once owned the property on which the *Lafayette Vineyards and Winery* is located. The vineyards, founded in 1983, specialize in wines from native Florida grapes. Tours and wine tastings are scheduled.

Location:	6505 Mahon Drive
Hours:	Monday through Saturday 10–6, Sunday 12–6, closed Thanksgiving, Christmas and New Year's Day
Fees:	No charge
Phone:	(800) 447–WINE

Heading South

The Tallahassee–St. Marks Railroad was Florida's oldest continuously operating railroad. It moved cotton and other products from the Northern Panhandle to the Port of St. Marks from 1837–1984. Although the tracks are gone, bicyclists, hikers, joggers, and horseback riders enjoy the eight–foot wide, 16–mile long *Tallahassee–St. Marks Historic Railroad State Trail* that follows the historic railroad bed. It is one of the safest bike trails in the state and is particularly enjoyable became it ends near the Marcos de Apalache State Historic Site in St. Marks.

Location:	Access via paved parking lot is located on SR 363 just South of SR 261 in Tallahassee or in the parking lot adjacent to the Marcos de Apalache State Historic Site in St. Marks

Woodville

From March 1–3, 1865, during the final weeks of the Civil War, a Union flotilla assembled in Apalachee Bay. The troops planned to march North, destroy Confederate supplies, and take Tallahassee by surprise.

The Panhandle was largely Confederate territory so it is not surprising that Tallahassee Confederates received an early warning of the planned attack. The call went out for volunteers.

Confederate volunteers and Union forces met at the *Natural Bridge Battlefield Historic Site*. Early in the morning of March 6, 1865, they fought along the natural bridge spanning the St. Mark's River. Before the day was over, there had been three attacks and several skirmishes. By early afternoon the Union forces had been defeated and began to retreat. On the following day they reached their flotilla and sailed back to Key West. The Battle at Natural Bridge kept Union troops from reaching Tallahassee and, many believe, kept the city from falling to Union troops.

Location:	Natural Bridge Road, 6 miles East of Woodville
Hours:	Daily 8–sunset
Fees:	No charge
Phone:	(904) 922–6007

Wakulla Springs

Old Indian legends tell of tiny water people who lived in Wakulla Springs. They were four inches tall and had long hair and held dances in the depths of the Springs on moonlit nights. At a certain hour, late at night, a mysterious warrior appeared in a stone canoe and frightened them away. Come to the Springs and see what you find!

Edward Ball Wakulla Springs State Park is the site of the world's deepest freshwater springs. The Indians called Wakulla Springs "Mysteries of Strange Water." Although the Springs usually flow at a rate of about 10,000 gallons per second, a record peak flow from the Spring was measured at 14,325 gallons per second in April 1973.

Its basin covers an area of four and a half–acres and reaches a maximum depth of 185–feet. The water is so clear that objects at the deepest point of the Springs are clearly visible. Because of the pristine setting, numerous Hollywood productions were filmed here, including some of the early Tarzan movies and *Creature from the Black Lagoon.*

Edward Ball, a conservationist, financier, member of the duPont family, and political figure bought the property. In 1937, he built a 27 room, Spanish–style lodge. The lodge, now the heart of the State Park property, is a fine place for a meal or an overnight stay. Particularly note the Tennessee marble floors, the blue heron fireplace andirons, the lobby ceiling, and the rafters with their handpainted Toltec and Aztec designs. The lodge has a limited number of guest rooms available—make reservations early! Or, just come for a swim, a glass–bottomed boat ride, and a jungle boat cruise down the river. All are fine ways to view waterlife, wildlife, lush vegetation, and to consider whether that shadow was really one of the legendary water people.

Location:	Wakulla Springs Road, Route 61, 13 miles South of Tallahassee
Hours:	Park 8–sunset
Fees:	Boat tour fees: Adult $4.50, children $2.25
Phone:	(904) 222–7279

St. Marks

The remains of a Spanish fort and mission are located at the *Marcos de Apalache State Historic Site.* Although Panfilo de Narvaez arrived in the area with 300 men in 1528, the Spanish did not begin building the Fort until 1679. The area was later occupied by English, Confederate, and Federal troops. Be sure to tour the Museum and climb the observation tower at the Wakulla River.

Location:	Canal Street, 1 mile Southwest of Route 363
Hours:	Thursday through Monday 9–5
Fees:	Adults and children over 6 $1
Phone:	(904) 925–6216

As mentioned earlier, the terminus of the Tallahassee–St. Marks Historic State Trail is in the parking lot for the Marcos de Apalache State Historic Site.

Early Tallahassee Bicyclists Enjoy an Afternoon Ride

Dixie Plantation,
Jefferson County

Monticello
Madison
Live Oak

Tour 22.
The
Tobacco
Road

The strong economic and political roots of this part of the state developed from the Civil War era. Confederate plantation owners came South to expand their holdings. The tour winds through small Southern towns whose antebellum architecture combines with history to provide an unusual tour.

Monticello

The town was founded by planters from Georgia and the Carolinas in the early 1800s. They built magnificent homes and planted the **Avenue of Oaks** in 1889. It is one of the main approaches to Monticello and provides a historic frame to the architecture, the landscaping, and the sense of an earlier Florida.

Wirick–Simmons House
Monticello

Madison

Transplanted Sea Island Cotton growers from South Carolina settled the town in 1838. First they planted, then they installed the world's largest long staple cotton gin. Cotton became the cash crop core of the community. In 1916 when there was a major boll weevil infestation, the economy was almost ruined. The rebuilding has been slow and many signs of the earlier times remain.

Although Confederate sympathies were strong throughout the Northern portion of the state, Madison and Monticello were particularly vocal in their views. When Florida seceded from the Union the townspeople were so pleased that they rang bells, built a bonfire, and had a party.

Confederate Square is at the heart of the community. The square was once the site of a blockhouse used as a refuge for women and children during the Seminole Indian War and was also a gathering place for sympathizers during the Civil War. Stop to read the plaques and tablets, and look at the monuments. If you're lucky, there might be a program scheduled at the bandstand.

Confederate Currency, dated June 2, 1862

Walk, browse, and drive slowly through this town to explore some of the residential area, the courthouse, and the shopping district.

Live Oak

The live oak came first, the town's name followed. There once was an old wagon road that ran from a military post at Suwannee Springs to the Gulf of Mexico. It passed a clear, deep pond under a huge live oak. Since the setting offered shade and a pretty camping ground, the area became known as Live Oak. When the railroad came through, the name became official.

For centuries parts of the Northern Panhandle have been known as tobacco growing regions. It was grown and smoked by Indians long before the appearance of European explorers. The first record of its use in the state appeared in a 1564 entry in the log of Captain John Hawkins, pirate and slave trader.

Tobacco was grown under slats. ca. 1910

In the 1890s, shade tobacco was introduced in the area. For many years, in order to sell their tobacco, Florida growers had to transport their leaf to auctions farther North.

Live Oak business people established a tobacco auction in their town to avoid the long trip to North Carolina.

As you drive into town, imagine that it is the first week in August early in the 20th century. The roads, of course, are still unpaved. The hot Florida summer sun shines through a hazy filter of dirt and dust. It is hot and people are everywhere. For weeks before the auction, farmers and their families—with wagons loaded with tobacco leaf—have been arriving from all directions.

There would have been a great sense of anticipation. The harvest was in and people were in a party mood. At times, the warehouse auction district looked like a carnival midway.

Owners took their burlap bags of tobacco into a warehouse where the tobacco was examined, weighed, and stacked in rows on the floor. Each stack was given a lot number, ticketed with the owner's name, and the total lot's weight was recorded. The owners then sat near their tobacco.

An auctioneer, surrounded by a cloud of buyers and observers, walked up and down the rows. The group stopped before each lot and the bidding began. The noise level rose as heated bidding occurred. If the owner was dissatisfied with the bid, the walking auction would pass by, leaving the owner to wait for the next day's auction to try for a better price.

When the auctioneer yelled "SOLD," there would be a flurry of activity. The buyer would have the burlap bags rapidly moved to nearby wagons, trucks, or railroad cars; the auction crew would clear the space, the next sellers would bring their tobacco into the warehouse, and the process would begin again.

Tobacco Auction 1965

North
Central
Florida

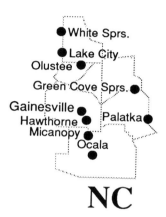

NC

Way Down Upon the Suwannee River is Florida's State Song. Although the composer had never seen the state or the river, his melodies and memories form the core of the **Suwannee River Tour**.

The **Thoroughbreds All** tour begins deep in steamboat country and continues to Ocala, an area noted for its thoroughbred horses, to Gainesville and its university and to Hawthorne to visit the home of Marjorie Kinnan Rawlings, author of **The Yearling**.

Mural in the Stephen Foster
State Folk Culture Center

White Sprs.
Lake City
Olustee

Tour 23.
A Composer
and the
Suwannee
River

White Springs

Indians considered the White Springs sacred. They marked trees in a five–mile circle around the Springs and warriors wounded in battle were not subject to attack as long as they recuperated within the boundaried area.

A white settlement was founded in 1826 on the North bank of the Suwannee River. By the turn of the century, the village and its Springs were known as a health resort and attracted many Northerners.

Around the time of the Civil War, the area became known as *Rebels Refuge*. Georgia and Carolina plantation owners moved here with their families and slaves trying to wait out the war in relative safety, out of the path of the Union invasion.

The *Stephen Foster State Folk Culture Center* is located on the banks of the Suwannee River. It honors the memory of American composer Stephen C. Foster who was born near Pittsburgh, Pennsylvania on July 4, 1826. One of America's best known musical storytellers, he wrote **The S'wanee River** (*Old Folks at Home*) in 1851 and sold it to famed minstrelman E. P. Christy. Mr. Foster went on to author about 200 songs during his prolific career.

It is tragic to realize that Stephen Foster, a man who brought so much music to the world, died alone in New York City. At his death, he was almost penniless.

While discussing his music, a moment must be taken to comment that Stephen Foster never, ever saw the Suwannee River. When he had finished composing *Old Folks at Home,* as the song was originally known, Stephen Foster was in Pittsburgh and asked his brother for some help.

When originally written, he had named it the Pee Dee, a South Carolina river. Mr. Foster talked to his brother about wanting a more musical sounding name and his brother pulled down an atlas. After the names of several Southern rivers were rejected, he looked at Florida's map. What about the Suwannee River (or as they spelled it, the S'wanee)? Perfect!

The Center combines a carillon, Stephen Foster exhibits, and displays of Florida folklife. Mr. Foster's melodies are played on the half hour and can be heard best from many of the quiet walking trails near the center and near the river.

Stephen Foster

Tour 23. Suwannee River – White Springs to Olustee – NC

Take a moment to gaze at the Suwannee River, listen to the carillon, perhaps hum a Stephen Foster melody, and silently thank this composer for his contribution to American music.

Location:	White Springs, off US 41 North
Hours:	**Park**: Daily 8–sunset. **Buildings**: Daily 9–5
Fees:	$3.25 per car, including up to 8 people per vehicle
Phone:	(904) 397-2733

Lake City

Florida's *Sports Hall of Fame* highlights the accomplishments of more than 100 nationally known athletes, coaches, and sports personalities. It is a perfect place to remember some of the great moments in American sports history.

Location:	201 Hall of Fame Drive
Hours:	Daily 9–9
Fees:	Donations welcome
Phone:	(904) 755-5666

Olustee

The major Florida Civil War conflict was fought at the *Olustee Battlefield*. On February 20, 1864, twelve regiments of Union troops engaged 5,000 Confederate soldiers. The story of the defeat of the Union troops is told in the museum on the grounds and the large monument is dedicated to those who fought and died here. Each February, a reenactment of the battle is held. Phone ahead for details.

Location:	2–1/2 miles East of Olustee on US 90
Hours:	**Battlefield**: daily 8–5. **Museum**: Thursday through Monday 8–5
Fees:	No charge
Phone:	(904) 752-3866

Green Cove Springs

Augusta Savage, the distinguished African–American sculptress, spent her childhood here. In the late 1870s and 1880s, Green Cove Springs was a fashionable winter resort. Steamboats from as far away as Charleston and Savannah travelled the St. Johns River and landed passengers at the resort piers. President Grover Cleveland and well–to–do Northerners came annually. Gail Borden, condensed milk manufacturer, and J.C. Penney, chain store magnate, bought property here and took active roles in the development of the town.

About eight miles away at Penney Farms, Mr. Penney built The *Penney Farms Memorial Community* to honor his parents. There are 96 apartments and a chapel. Dedicated in 1927, this is a home for retired religious leaders of all denominations.

While in Green Cove Springs, drive past *St. Mary's Church* which was built in 1878. It is one of the best examples of Carpenter Gothic architecture in the state and is located on St. John's Avenue.

Palatka

Palatka developed as an early trading and lumbering town. During the Civil War, it was occupied by Union troops. After the war, like Green Cove Springs, it also became a fashionable Winter resort. Easterners would travel by train to Jacksonville and then take the steamboat to town. In its heyday, there were nine resort hotels, including the Putnam House with 400 rooms. It was also a political center where many of the prominent Florida politicians of the era lived or visited.

Bronson–Mulholland House is a three–story cypress plantation–style home with Greek Revival lines. It was built for Judge Isaac Bronson, one of Florida's major political figures and one of the state's first circuit riders.

Location:	100 Mulholland Park, Highway 17 at Reed Street
Hours:	Tuesdays, Thursdays, and Sundays, 2–5
Fees:	No charge
Phone:	(904) 329–0140

During the 1930s, one of the area's WPA projects was the planting of over 70,000 azaleas and thousands of subtropical trees and shrubs at the *Ravine State Gardens*. Today's displays are magnificent, particularly in February and March.

Be careful as you cross one of the two *Swinging Bridges* across the ravine. Once you, or your teenager, start the bridge swinging, it will continue to give you a frightening walk until you reach the other side.

On a more sedate note, the *Court of Flags*, another WPA project, is composed of 50 columns of limestone from which all U.S. State flags are flown on public holidays.

Location:	1600 Twigg Street
Hours:	Daily, 8–sunset
Fees:	$3.25 per car, including up to 8 people per vehicle
Phone:	(904) 329–3721

Dating from the early 1850s, *St. Mark's Episcopal Church* was designed by Richard Upjohn, architect of New York's Trinity Church. During the Civil War, Union troops used it as their shelter. Although it is not open to the public, it is an interesting example of church building of the period and is located at 200 Main Street.

Ocala

Ocala is at the center of some of the finest horse country in the nation. There are about 600 horse farms in the state, with about 75% of them in the Ocala–Marion County area and the equine industry is a $1 billion business employing more than 29,000 people.

Over the past decade, Ocala horse breeding and training farms have produced five Kentucky Derby winners and the state ranks third in the nation in thoroughbred breeding.

Drive along scenic highway 301. One of the reasons there are so many horse farms in the area is the high quality of the grass. Water is naturally filtered through layers of limestone, providing trace minerals which help develop the animals' strong bones. If you visit in the autumn, it is possible to simply stop along the fence posts and watch these animals being exercised and trained—and watch them watching you.

Florida Thoroughbreds

Appleton Museum of Art houses a collection spanning 5,000 years. There are excellent pieces from the Orient, South and Central America as well as fine glassware.

Location:	4333 East Silver Springs Boulevard
Hours:	Tuesday through Saturday 10–4:30, Sunday 1–5
Fees:	Adults $3, children $2
Phone:	(904) 236–5050

Don Garlits was one of the major pioneers of drag racing and developed and raced the rear engine, top fueled dragster. The *Don Garlits' Museum of Drag Racing* features racing exhibits and memorabilia as well as a vintage collection of drag racers.

Location:	13700 Southwest 16th Avenue, 8 miles South of Ocala
Hours:	Daily 9–5:30, closed Christmas Day
Fees:	Adults $6, children 3–12 $3
Phone:	(904) 245–8661

The *Florida Hall of Fame* has been established by the Florida Thoroughbred Breeder's Association. It is an impressive starting point to learn more about the industry and is also a good place to ask about horse farms open for public visits.

Location:	4727 Northwest 80th Avenue, 7 miles West of Ocala
Hours:	Monday through Friday, 9–5
Fees:	No charge
Phone:	(904) 629–2160

Micanopy

Once the site of an Indian village, Micanopy is one of Florida's oldest towns. The community is now attracting artists and artisans to its historic district. In 1991, a romantic comedy entitled *Doc Hollywood,* starring Michael J. Fox, was released. Look carefully at the downtown parade scenes. Parts of the film were shot on location in Micanopy.

Hawthorne

M arjorie Kinnan Rawlings came to Florida's Cracker Country and stayed to lovingly record many of its strengths and frailties.

Marjorie Kinnan Rawlings at Work in Hawthorne

Mrs. Rawlings' Florida career began when she sold a Florida Cracker story to *Scribner's Magazine* in the late 1920s. Maxwell Perkins, who also mentored Ernest Hemingway, liked her work and encouraged her to continue writing about the isolation of the pioneer farm families in this part of Florida. She stayed in Hawthorne and wrote about families in Florida's back country.

From her vantage point on Cross Creek, Mrs. Rawlings told of her love of the land and shared the touching, classic story of *The Yearling*. She won the hearts of readers everywhere, as well as a Pulitzer Prize for that work.

The *Marjorie Kinnan Rawlings State Historic Site* permits visitors to tour the author's home, remember her works, and learn more about an important era of Florida's development.

Location:	Off County Road 325
Hours:	Thursday through Monday, guided tours are provided on the half–hour from 10–11:30 and 1–4:30 on a first come, first served basis only, closed Tuesdays and Wednesdays, Thanks–giving, Christmas, and New Year's Day
Fees:	Adults $2, children 6–12 $1
Phone:	(904) 466–3672

Gainesville

It is hard to look around today's Gainesville and realize that residents once graced it with the name *Hog Town*. As the community grew, they realized the name was no longer appropriate and renamed the town to honor General Edmund Gaines who had captured Aaron Burr and was the victorious commander of the Second Seminole War.

Bring the kids and plan to spend an afternoon at one of the top ten natural history museums in the country. The *Florida Museum of Natural History* is an outstanding resource for learning more about the rich and varied history of the state. Of particular interest for children is the Fossil Study Center, an interactive learning environment where kids can find prehistoric skeletons or go on a fossil hunt using a computer to plot their strategy.

Some of the prehistoric animals that r o a m e d what is now Florida

Location:	Museum Road and Newell Drive on the University of Florida campus
Hours:	Tuesday through Saturday 10–4, Sunday and holidays 1–4, closed Christmas
Fees:	No charge
Phone:	(904) 392–1721

The *University Library* has an excellent collection of the works, writings, and papers of many of Florida's authors including three members of Florida's *Writer's Hall of Fame*: Zora Neale Houston, John D. MacDonald, and Marjorie Kinnan Rawlings. Another major reason to visit the Library is the *Creative Writing Manuscript Collection* which shows the writing process through drafts, edits, and changes of the works of hundreds of writers, including Truman Capote.

Location:	Smathers Library East on the University of Florida Campus
Hours:	Monday to Friday, 10–5. Closed state holidays
Fees:	No charge
Phone:	(904) 392–0321

Starting in the early 1880s, the *Devil's Millhopper State Geological Site* has been a tourist attraction. It is an 120–foot deep sinkhole, probably the largest in the State since it covers a five–acre area.

Take the walkway and descend into the sinkhole. Some of the items found in this hole have included fossil shark teeth and fossilized remains of extinct land animals—some of which are now displayed in the nearby Florida Museum of Natural History.

Location:	Off State Road 23
	2 miles NW
Hours:	Daily 9–sunset
Fees:	$3.25 per car, including up to 8 people per vehicle
Phone:	(904) 336–2008

Make time to walk into a 62 acre woodland complete with meadows, butterflies and hummingbirds. The *Kapaha Botanical Gardens* were established in 1978 and contain one of the largest bamboo collections in the Southeast.

Location:	4625 Southwest 63rd Boulevard
Hours:	Monday, Tuesday, and Friday 9–5, Wednesday, Saturday, and Sunday 9–sunset.
Fees:	Adults $1.50, children 6–12 75¢
Phone:	(904) 372–4981

We end the uncommon tours portion of the book with a remarkable visit for you.

After you have spent time at the *Paynes Prairie State Preserve,* the state may never look quite the same to you. Florida's State Park System and the Department of Natural Resources have done a near perfect job maintaining the prairie in its historic condition.

When you hike along the trails, realize the Preserve is one of only a few locations preserved as the area would have seemed to the earliest settlers, explorers, and Indians. Imagine a herd of buffalo, much larger than the herd you will see, running free across the prairie, perhaps being hunted by an Indian tribe.

The Visitor Center has exhibits and an audiovisual program to increase your appreciation and enjoyment of the area. The hiking trails are first–rate.

Location:	US 441, 10 miles South of Gainesville
Hours:	Daily 8–sunset
Fees:	$3.25 per car, including up to 8 people
Phone:	(904) 466–3397

See the Buffalo Herd at the Paynes Prairie State Preserve

Annual
Events

Florida has an uncommon number of unusual and interesting annual events. In this section, we share over 60 of the roughly 500 special yearly activities which occur across the state. We urge you to include a few of these in your travel plans and to search out your own favorites.

January

Art Deco Weekend brings together bands, antiques, and tours in one of the state's outstanding 20th century architectural areas. Miami Beach, SE, (305) 672–2014.

The *Festival of the Epiphany* includes Greek entertainment and the blessing of the fleet as part of a colorful celebration observing Christ's baptism. Tarpon Springs, SW, (813) 937–3540.

February

In the old days, Jose Gaspar—a pirate known as Gasparilla—terrified ship captains in Florida's waters. For the *Gaspiralla Festival*, he and his Mystic Krewe return for the month–long party which combines history with a vast array of contemporary festival events. Of particular interest is *Fiesta Day* held in the *Ybor City* district. Tampa, Ybor City, SW, (813) 228–7338.

If you only schedule a visit to one fair during the year, make it the *Florida State Fair*. Each year, there are county exhibits highlighting a part of the state's history, a living history farm exhibit, competitions and entertainment activities. Tampa, SW, (813) 621–7821.

Festival of Lights commemorates Thomas Alva Edison, the inventor of the electric light. Although the city–wide ceremonies last for two weeks, if you want to be authentic, plan to go on February 11 which was Mr. Edison's birthday. Fort Myers, SW, (813) 334–2550.

February is harvest month for citrus and strawberries. Plan a visit to Central Florida to enjoy the *Florida Citrus Festival*. It is a 10–day event which highlights all of Florida's citrus products. Expect to see fruit competitions and exhibits as well as a wide variety of entertainment in—what else?—The Orange Dome. Winter Haven, C, (813) 293–3175.

The strawberry capital of the country is located between Tampa and Orlando, just off I–4. Make time to see the exhibits and enjoy a piece of strawberry shortcake at the *Florida Strawberry Festival*. Plant City, C, (813) 752–9194.

The *Sistrunk Historical Festival* celebrates African–American and Caribbean cultures with an emphasis on family entertainment, food, and crafts. Fort Lauderdale, SE, (305) 765–4269.

The *Mount Dora Art Festival* is one of the largest juried shows in the state. Mount Dora, C, (904) 383–0880.

Silver Spurs Rodeo is a fine place to watch steer wrestling and calf roping. Kissimmee, C, (407) 628–2280.

Celebrate Spring in Japanese fashion at the *Hatsume Spring Festival* at the Morikami Museum of Japanese Culture. You will see Japanese performing arts and bonsai exhibits as well as touring the gardens. The festival's name means "first bud of the New Year." Delray Beach, SE, (407) 495–0233.

Each year, Henry Flagler's mansion is the site of a free, opulent party. Make plans to attend the *Annual Open House at Whitehall*. The grounds will be filled with classic cars and other reminders of the early 20th century. Listen to piano and organ recitals, see films, and explore the home of Florida's major empire builder. Palm Beach, SE, (407) 655–2833.

The Civil War had a tremendous impact on Northern Florida and across the Panhandle. The *Olustee Battle Festival* includes the second–largest Civil War reenactment in the U.S., the largest being Gettysburg. Plan a visit to see the battle reenacted, be part of the memorial service, and admire the fine work at the crafts festival. Olustee, NC, (904) 755–5666.

Sound never stops during *Daytona's Speed Weeks* The activities include 24–hour races and stock car races. Daytona, EC, (904) 253–RACE.

March

Soon after the car races do stop, the motorcycle races begin. Lasting 10 days, *Daytona's Bike Week* features motorcycle races, awards, honors, and grandstand shows. Daytona, EC, (904) 253-RACE.

Staying on the automotive theme, the 12–hour *Endurance Race*, the country's oldest auto race, is held at the world famous Sebring International Raceway. The race is one of four world class races that test for the world leader in speed and endurance. Sebring, C, (813) 655–1442.

One of the last battles of the Civil War occurred at the Natural Bridge on March 6, 1865. It was here that Confederate troops defended Tallahassee from Union soldiers. Although the Natural Bridge State Historic Site is interesting at any time of the year, plan a visit for the *Battle of Natural Bridge Reenactment*. Woodville, NP, (904) 925–6216.

Spend a few days at the *Annual Sanibel Shell Fair* learning more about the wide variety of shells which find their way to the island. Sanibel Island, SW, (813) 472–1080.

We've talked about Calle Ocho, an area in Miami's Little Havana district. Plan to spend a few days at *Carnival Miami*, the largest and most colorful Hispanic festival in the country. It lasts for nine days and includes arts, crafts, foods, shows, and a world class parade. Miami, SE, (305) 324–7349.

At least once, make your way to *McGuire's St. Patrick's Day Celebration,* one of the largest events of its kind in the U.S. Add a Mc or a Pat to your name, wear green, and practice your brogue before taking part in this holiday. Pensacola, GC, (904) 433–6789.

Strolling minstrels at a *Medieval Fair* seem perfectly right on the grounds of the John and Mable Ringling Museum of Art. Sarasota, SE, (813) 355–5101.

Indian tribes from across the country meet for an *Annual Pow Wow* which features arts, crafts, and Indian dancing. Fort Myers, SW, (813) 455–2171.

Flowers, parades, and contests highlight a month of activities during *Springtime Tallahassee.* The major festival combines a celebration of the city's founding with children's events, hot air balloons, music, and more. Tallahassee, NP, (904) 224–1373.

April

If you love a parade, come to the *Festival of States* where bands from around the nation compete. Music fills the air throughout the area since the *Sam Robinson Jazz Festival* is also held during the 17–day festival period. St. Petersburg, SW, (813) 898–3546.

The first mass in what is now the U.S. was celebrated in St. Augustine. Beginning on Palm Sunday and continuing through Easter Sunday plan to take part in the *Easter Festival*, watch the Passion Play, and appreciate the historic setting. St. Augustine, NE (904) 829–5681.

Enjoy the *International Bok Tower Carillon Festival* when carillonneurs from around the world share their favorite music in the peaceful garden setting. Lake Wales, C, (813) 676–1408.

The *Lunar Festival* commemorates the Koreshan religious sect founded by Cyrus Teed. Arts, crafts, and tours are also featured on the grounds of the Koreshan State Historic Site. Estero, SW, (813) 992–0311.

Paynes Prairie State Preserve reflects how Florida used to look. It is particularly special to see the area on *William Bartram Day* when crafts displays, interpretive tours, and pioneer exhibits enhance the natural beauty of the setting. Gainesville, NC, (904) 372–4305.

Don't miss the *Blue Angels Annual Air Show* at the Naval Air Station's Cecil Field. Jacksonville, GC, (904) 778–6055.

May

Seafood festivals can be found across Florida. One of our favorites is the *Isle of Eight Flags Shrimp Festival.* Combine historic buildings with a day of good eating and learning more about the important shrimp fleets. Fernandina Beach on Amelia Island, NE, (904) 261–3248.

Staying with the food theme, don't miss the *Florida Blueberry Festival.* It is suggested that you arrive hungry and be prepared to eat too many of the delicious treats waiting for you. Arts, crafts, jazz, and bluegrass are also part of the activities. Ocala, C, (904) 237–3247.

There is nothing quite like fresh, steamed corn on the cob particularly when it is prepared at the *Zellwood Sweet Corn Festival*. Besides the all–you–can–eat ears of corn, there are also arts, crafts, and competitions at a festival which commemorates the Indian planting of maize. Zellwood, C, (904) 886–0014.

Refresh your eyes and your soul with a trip to the *Orchid Festival Week* at the Selby Botanical Gardens. Sarasota, SW, (813) 366–5730.

Masaryktown is an early Florida community which was largely settled by Czechs. Plan on an interesting day as they share their heritage at the *Arts, Crafts, and Music Festival*. Masaryktown, SW, (904) 796–5027.

The *Fiesta of Five Flags* reflects Pensacola's heritage. Don Tristan de Luna, the city's Spanish founder, retakes the city in a week of festivities that also reflect the French, British, Confederate, and American occupations. Pensacola, GC, (904) 433–6512.

The *Florida Folk Festival* is a must–see event. Held at the Stephen Foster State Folk Culture Center, it is a magnificent blend of craftspeople, traditional musicians, storytellers, and food providers in a beautiful setting. The Festival celebrates the folk songs, music, dance, legends, crafts, and other forms of traditional expression that reflect the folklife of Florida and is sponsored by the Florida Department of State. White Springs, NC, (904) 397-2192.

There's a lot of hot air during a Florida summer. One of the best ways to enjoy it is with a trip to the *Fred Bondesan Central Florida Balloon Classic*. The weekend activities combine ballooning, skydiving, classic cars, and World War II aircraft exhibitions. DeLand, C, (904) 734–4331.

June

Bahamians were early settlers on the Florida Keys and the South Coast of Florida. Don't miss the *Goombay Festival* which adds a Bahamian feeling to an art fair with parade, food booths, and music. Coconut Grove, SE, (305) 444–7270.

June is watermelon month across the Northern Panhandle. Plan a visit to the *Jefferson County Watermelon Festival* for more delicious melon–related activities than can be imagined. Monticello, NP, (904) 997–5552.

If it were only possible to spend two evenings in St. Augustine, I'd go to the *Spanish Night Watch Weekend*. Soldiers from the Castillo reenact a battle, musicians in 18th century dress stroll through the town, and craftspeople share their skills in the Old City. Bring a candle to light the way of the historic processional through the town. Stay an extra day to see the *Cross and Sword*, Florida's state play which is shown in an outdoor amphitheater and tells the story of St. Augustine's founding. The play shows nightly through the summer. St. Augustine, NE. Details for Spanish Night Watch Weekend, (904) 829–9792 and for *Cross and Sword*, (904) 824–1965.

Loggerhead turtles often weigh more than 250 pounds and lay their eggs along the state's East Coast beaches. Evening *turtle walks* are offered by a number of state and naturalist groups. For details contact the following: Gumbo Limbo Nature Center in Boca Raton, EC, (407) 338–1473; Florida Power and Light in Fort Pierce, EC, (800) 552–8440; Blowing Rocks Audubon Preserve at Jupiter Inlet, EC, (407) 575–2297, or the Sebastian Inlet State Park, EC, (407) 984–4852.

July

Most Florida communities celebrate the *Fourth of July*. Almost all of the celebrations are a fine way to spend the holiday. However, several of the Independence Day celebrations are major events in their own right. At the risk of leaving out dozens of other outstanding activities, we highlight *EPCOT Center's* special *IllumiNations* show; the *Ethnic Food Festival* and fireworks which are part of Jacksonville's July 4th celebrations; and the

Miami Beach Jazz Carnival's fireworks held in a Mardi Gras setting. Details for EPCOT, Lake Buena Vista, C, (407) W–DISNEY; Ethnic Food Festival's Fireworks, Jacksonville, NE, (904) 396–4900; Miami Beach Jazz Carnival, Miami and Miami Beach, SE, (305) 571–1515.

Ernest Hemingway lives on during the *Hemingway Days Festival.* Two important features of these activities are the storytelling contest and the Ernest Hemingway look–alike contest. Be prepared. Key West, SW, (305) 294–4440.

August

The *Florida International Festival* brings world–class musicians to Daytona Beach each year. Listen to the London Symphony Orchestra and enjoy the city's *SummerFaire.* Daytona Beach, EC, (904) 255–1314.

There are sand castles and sand castles. Each year the master architects of the art form compete at the annual *Sand Castle Contest.* Naples, SW, (813) 597–1666.

Ocalifest highlights native Florida food and cultures, including reenactments of skirmishes between Seminoles and the militia. Ocala, NC, (904) 629–8406.

September

Watch Hernando de Soto and his conquistadors come ashore to take part in the *Fiesta de San Marcos.* St. Marks, NP, (904) 925–6224.

Seafood festivals continue through September and October. Head for the *Seafood Festival* where Gulf Coast shrimp, mullet, shark, arts, crafts, and history featured. Pensacola, GC, (904) 433–6512.

Central American Independence Day is celebrated at Bayfront Park. Miami, SE, (305) 541–7677.

October

During *Ocala Week*, there are parties and other activities surrounding the major event, the *Annual Fall Mixed Racehorse Sale*. Ocala, NC, (904) 629–2160.

The *Hispanic Heritage Festival* tells of Hispanic cultural contributions to Florida through arts, crafts, folklure, and food. Miami, SE, (305) 541–5023.

Polish bands, dancing, foods, arts, and crafts are part of the annual *Polish Festival*. Titusville, EC, (904) 267–4111.

Seafood is king during the *Indian Summer Seafood Festival*. Panama City Beach, GC, (800) PCBEACH.

Some of America's best jazz can be heard during the three–day *Jacksonville Jazz Festival*. Besides hearing some of the all time greats perform, be sure to listen to the Great American Jazz Piano Competition. You'll drive home humming. Jacksonville, NE, (904) 353–7770.

Cedar Key is one of our favorite quiet hideaways. However, all that changes during the *Seafood Festival* when artists and craftspeople converge along with an amazing variety of seafood. Cedar Key, GC, (904) 543–5410.

November

The Gulf Coast and great seafood go together. The *Florida Seafood Festival* is a month–long festival. Apalachicola, GC, (904) 653–8051. While on the Gulf Coast, also plan to enjoy the *Great Gulfcoast Arts Festival* which brings together artists and craftspeople from across the country. Pensacola, GC, (904) 432–9906.

Enjoy an afternoon in a small town at the *Micanopy Country Festival*. Music, dancing, arts, crafts, and antiques are all part of the activities. Micanopy, NC, (904) 466–4789.

From the variety of Florida's gardens, many people believe almost anything will grow in the state. Plan a visit to the *Annual Flower Show of the Lake County Council of Garden Clubs* and be astonished at the beauty and variety of the offerings. Eustis, C, (904) 357–3136.

December

Lights fill the nights and reflect off the water during several holiday season boat parades. Travel to Fort Lauderdale where over a hundred magnificently decorated boats travel the Intracoastal Waterway with parties and concerts ashore and afloat during the *Winterfest and Boat Parade*. Fort Lauderdale, SE, (305) 765–4466. Nearby, the *Winter Fantasy on the Waterway* combines a boat parade with music and fireworks. Boca Raton, SE, (305) 395–4433.

Don't miss the torchlight procession which is part of the *Grand Illumination* festival. Plan on carol singing, fife and drum performances, and a better understanding of the long reach of Florida's history. St. Augustine, NE, (904) 829–5681.

Index

— A —

A–7, 164
Advanced Redoubt, 164
Air
— Conditioning, 153
— Force Space Museum, 44
Alcazar Hotel, 28
Alfred B. Maclay State Gardens, 173
Alfonso XIII, King of Spain, 121
Amelia Island, 12–14, 141
— Plantation, 15
American
— Lighthouse Museum, 21
— Police Hall of Fame and
Museum, 68
Anastasia
— Island, 29–30
— Limestone, 51
— State Recreation Area, 30
Ancient Spanish Monastery, 71–72
Anheuser–Busch Brewery, 18
Animal
— Exploratorium, 67
— Olympics, 136
— Shows, 110
Animation Tour, 102
Annie Pfeiffer Chapel, 111
Annual
— Fall Mixed Racehorse Sale, 206
— Flower Show of the Lake
County Council of Garden
Clubs, 207
— Open House at Whitehall, 200
— Pow Wow, 201
— Sanibel Shell Fair, 201
Apalachee Indians, 151, 174
Apalachicola, 151–154
— Bay, 151, 177
— — Oysters, 152

— River, 169
Appleton Museum of Art, 193
Architects
— Graves, Michael, 105
— Isozaki, Arato, 105
— Merrick, George, 73–75
— Mizner, Addison, 56, 58–59
— Nolan, John, 132
— Olmstead, Jr., Frederick Law,
113
— Schulze and Weaver, 57
— Schweizer, Nils, 111
— Stern, Robert A. M., 105
— Stone, Edward Durrell, 108, 172
— Upjohn, Richard, 191
— Wood, John A., 118
— Wright, Frank Lloyd, 94, 97,
111
Architecture
— Antebellum, 125
— Art Deco, 70
— Bahamian, 89
— Baroque, 129
— Carpenter Gothic, 190
— Cracker, 136
— Creole, 163
— Disney, 105
— French Creole, 162
— French Renaissance, 129
— Greek Revival, 162, 169, 191
— Gothic, 57
— Italian Renaissance, 56, 129
— Modern, 129
— Queen Anne, 169
— Renaissance, 229
— Renaissance Revival, 162
— Spanish, 162
— Steamboat Gothic, 100

— Venetian Gothic, 129
— Venetian Victorian, 96, 97
— Victorian, 142, 163, 166
Arming the Air Force, 158
Art Deco
— District, 70
— Weekend
Artists
— Audubon, John James, 91
— Bartlett, Frederick and Evelyn, 61
— Bearden, Romare, 119
— Catlin, George, 24
— Dali, Salvadore, 122–123
— Jones, Lois Marilou, 119
— Lalique, René, 97
— Parrish, Maxfield, 97
— Remington, Frederic, 108, 118
— Rubens, Peter Paul, 129–130
— Savage, Augusta, 190
— Smith, Jules André, 98
— Tanner, Henry, 119
— Tiffany, Louis Comfort, 28, 97
Arts, Crafts, and Music Festival, 203
Astronaut Memorial, 31, 37, 43
— Space Science Center and Planetarium, 45
Atlantic Coastline Railroad, 140
Audubon
— Aviary
— House and Garden, 91
— John James, 91
— Society, 47
Authors
— Capote, Truman, 196
— Crane, Stephen, 41
— Douglas, Marjory Stoneman, 77
— Hemingway, Ernest, 90–91
— Hurston, Zora Neale, 98, 196
— Lindberg, Anne Morrow, 138
— MacDonald, John D., 196
— Rawlings, Marjorie Kinnan, 185, 194, 196
Authors' Room, Key West, 92

Avenue of Oaks, 181

— B —

B–28 Bomber, 158
Bagdad, 166
Bacall, Lauren, 84
Backstage Tour, 102
Back to the Future Ride, 110
Baggs, Bill, 82
Bahama Channel, 87
Bald Cypress, 99
Baleen Whale Skeleton, 112
Ball, Edward, 177–178
Bannister, Edward, 119
Barefoot Mailman, 52
Barker, Ma, 100
Barnacle State Historic Site, 73
Barnacles, 73
Bartlett
— Evelyn, 61
— Frederick Clay, 61
— Helen Birch, 61
Barton, Clara, 119
Bass Museum of Art, 70
Battle
— at Natural Bridge, 177
— of Natural Bridge Reenactment, 201
Bayfront Park, 67
Bayside, 68
Bearden, Romare, 119
Belleview Biltmore Hotel, 141
Belle Vista Plantation, 33
Benjamin, Confederate Secretary Judah P., 125–126
Bethesda–by–the–Sea, 57
Bethune–Cookman College, 38–39
Bethune, Dr. Mary McLeod, 38–39
Bicycle Trails
— Palm Beach, 57
— Tallahassee to St. Marks, 176, 179

Big
— Pine Key, 88–89
— Thunder Mountain Railroad,
    103
— Tree Park, 99
Bill Baggs Cape Florida State Park,
    72
Birthplace of Speed Museum, 34
Biscayne
— Bay, 76
— National Underwater Park, 77,
    79
Bishop Planetarium, 127
Black Archives Museum and
    Research Center, 172
Blackbeard, 85–86
Black
— Caesar, 85–86
— Caesar's Rock, 85–86
Blitzen Benz, 32
Blowing Rocks Audubon Preserve,
    51, 204
Bloxham, Governor William, 107
Blue Angels, 163–164, 202
— Annual Air Show, 202
Bluebird, 34
Boca Raton, 58–59, 204, 206
— Hotel and Club, 59
Bogart, Humphry, 84
Bok, Edward, 94, 113
Bok Tower Garden, 113–114
Bondesan, Fred, 203
Bonnet House, 61
Bonus Army, 86
Borden, Gail, 190
Bowles, William Augustus, 151
Boy From Mars, 44
Boy Scouts, 35
Bradenton, 136
Bradley's Country Store, 176
Breakers, 56
Brevard Art Center and Museum, 46
Bristol, 149–150
Bronson, Judge Isaac, 191
Bronson–Mulholland House, 191

Brooksville, 145
Brotherhood of Locomotive Engi-
    neers, 132
Burr, Aaron, 195
Busch Gardens, 120
Butterfly World, 63

— *C* —

Cade, J. J., 54
Ca'd'Zan, 128–129
Calhoun Street Historic District, 173
Calle Ocho, Miami, 69, 201
Calusa Indians, 107
Campbell, Sir Malcomb, 34
Canaveral, 45
— National Seashore, 45
Canopy Roads, 175
Caparaca, 40
Cape
— Canaveral, 21
— — Air Force Station, 44
— Florida Lighthouse, 72
Capote, Truman, 196
Captiva Island, 138
Carlisle Indian School, 25
Carnival Miami, 201
Casements, 34–35
Casting Center, 105
Castillo de San Marcos, 23–25
Castle St. Mark, 23
Catlin, George, 24
Cecil Field, 202
Cedar Key, 116, 141, 147, 206
— Historical Society Museum, 147
— State Museum, 147
Center for the Fine Arts, Miami, 66
Center Street Restoration, 13
Centerville, 176
Central
— American Independence Day,
    206
— Florida Zoological Park, 99
Charles Deering Estate, 76

Chautauqua, 167
Chekika,
— Chief, 79
— Raid, 79
— State Recreation Area, 79
Child of the Sun Collection, 111
Children's Museum, 59
Churchill, Winston, 119
Church Street Station, 97
Cigar Worker's Home, 121
Circus Galleries, 131
City Gates, St. Augustine,
City of Jacksonville Sidewheeler, 20
City Pier, Panama City Beach, 156
Civil War, 12–13, 15, 24, 30, 92,
    125–126, 139, 147, 154, 161,
    164, 169, 172, 177, 181–182,
    187, 189–191, 200
Clearwater, 141–142
—Marine ScienceCenter,
    Aquarium and Museum, 142
Cleveland, President Grover, 190
Cluett Memorial Garden, 57
Coca–Cola, 169
Cocoa, 45
Coconut
— Creek, 63
— Grove, 72–73
Collier
— Automotive Museum, 139
— County Museum, 139
Columns, 172
Congo River Rapids, 120
Columbus, Christopher, 68
Confederate Square, 167
Constitution Convention State
    Museum, 153—154
Coolidge, President Calvin, 113
Coquina Stone, 23, 30
Corbin Lock Company, 34
Coral Castle, 80
Coral Gables, 73–74
— City Hall, 74
— House, 74
Court of Flags, 191

Cow Town, 108
Crane
— Point Hammock, 88
— Stephen, 41
Creation Door, 114
Creature from the Black Lagoon,
    178
Creative Writing Manuscript
    Collection, 196
Creek Indian, 151
Crescent, 71
Cristy, E.P., 187
Cross, 71
Cross and Sword, 30, 204
Cuesta–Rey Cigar Factory, 121
Cummer Gallery of Art, 19
Cypress Gardens, 94, 115

— D —

Dali, Salvador, 122—123
Darling, J. N. "Ding", 137—138
Daytona, 38, 200
—Beach, 37—39, 41, 205
—International Speedway, 38
—— Bike Weeks, 200
—— Speed Weeks, 200
Deering, Charles, 76
Deering, James, 67
DeFuniak Springs, 167—168
DeLand, 100, 203
DeLand, Henry A., 100
Delray Beach, 58, 200
DeLuna, Don Tristan, 203
Del Valle, José Cecello, 68
Demons, Peter, 122
De Narváez, Panfilo, 178
Departure of Lot, 129—130
Deseret Ranch, 46
De Soto
— Canyon, 157
— Hernando, 127, 174
—National Monument, 127
Destin, 157
Deusenberg, 139

Devil's Millhopper State Geological
    Site, 196
Dickinson, Jonathan, 50
Discovery Center Museum, 61
Discovery Island, 104
Disney–MGM Studios, 102
Disney, Flora and Elias, 107
Disney, Walt, 107, 115
Disston, Hamilton, 107
Doc Hollywood, 193
Dolphin Hotel, 105
Doolittle, General James, 158
Don Garlits Museum of Drag
    Racing, 193
Donnelly House, 100
Dorr House, 162
Douglas, Marjory Stoneman, 77
Dream
    — *is Alive*, 44
    — *of Empire, A Struggle to
    Survive*, 25
Dr. Thunder's Magic Boom Ride,
    120

— E —

Earthquake, 110
East
    — Coast Railroad, 34, 77, 80, 83
    — Martello Museum and Art
    Gallery, 92
    — Tohopekaliga Lake, 107
Easter Festival, 202
Eatonville, 98
Edison
    — Thomas Alva, 125, 134–135,
    199
    — Winter Home, Gardens, and
    Museum, 135
Edward Ball Wakulla Springs State
    Park, 177—178
Eglin Air Force Base, 158
Ellenton, 125—126
Elliott Museum, 49

Elliott, Sterling, 49
Ellis A. Gimbel Garden for the
    Blind, 67
Embry–Riddle University, 38
Endurance Race, 200
EPCOT Center, 102—103, 204
Estero, 139, 202
    — River, 139
Ethnic Food Festival, 204
Eustis, 207
Everglades
    — National Park, 24, 53, 63, 77–79
Everglades, River of Grass, 77

— F —

F–4, 164
F–104 Starfighter, 158
F–105 Thunderchief, 158
Fairchild Tropical Garden, 73
Fantasia Fireworks, 102
Farewell to Arms, A, 90
Farmers Market, 18
Ferdinand IV, King of Spain, 161
Ferlita Bakery, 121
Fernandina Beach, 12, 202
Festival of
    — Lights, 199
    — States, 201
    — the Epiphany, 198
Fiesta
    — Day, 198
    — of Five Flags, 203
Firestone, Henry, 135
Fine Arts Gallery and Museum, 173
Fire Station #3, 96
Fisher, Carl, 69—70
Fisher, Mel, 126
Flagler, Henry, 25—26, 28—29, 34,
    54—57, 60, 66, 77, 83—84,
    111, 117, 200
Florida
    — A & M University, 172
    — Blueberry Festival, 202

— Caverns State Park, 168
— Citrus Festival, 199
— City, 80
— Folk Festival, 203
— International Festival, 205
— Keys, 83–92
— Museum of Natural History, 195–196
— Panther, 79, 173
— Pioneer Museum, 80
— Power and Light Company, 204
— Seafood Festival, 206
— Southern College, 111—112
— State
—— Fair, 199
—— Farmer's Market, 80
— Strawberry Festival, 199
— Thoroughbred Breeder's Association, 193
Florida, State of
— Archives, 20, 175
Flying Tigers Warbird Air Museum, 108
Ford
— Henry, 125, 135—136
— Winter Home, 136
Forest Capital State Museum, 149
Fort
— Barrancas, 164
— Clinch State Park, 13—14
— Gadsden State Historic Site,149
— George Island, 15—16
— Lauderdale, 60—63, 199, 207
— Myers, 125, 134—136, 199, 201
—— Historical Museum, 136
— Pickens, 158
— Pierce, 204
— Walton
—— Beach, 157
—— Indian Culture, 157
For Whom the Bell Tolls , 90
Foster, Stephen, 20, 186—189
Fountain of Youth, 27—28
Four Evangelists, 130
Foxahatchee River, 50—51

Fox, Michael J., 193
Freedom Tower, 68
Fred Bondesan Central Florida Balloon Classic, 203
Fuller's Earth, 169

— G —

Gaines, General Edmund, 195
Gainesville, 145, 185, 195—197, 202
Gallery of Space Flight Museum, 44
Gamble
— Major Robert, 125
— Plantation State Historic Site and Memorial to J. B. Ben–jamin, 125—126
Garlits, Don, 193
Gaspar, José, 'Gasparilla,' 133, 138, 198
Gasparilla
— Festival, 198
— Island, 133
Gatorland Zoo, 109
Geiger, Captain John, 91
Gemini Program, 44
Geronimo, 158
Gift from the Sea, 138
Gilbert's Bar House of Refuge, 50
Gillespie Museum of Minerals, 100
Gimbel, Ellis A., 67
Glenn, John, 45
God's Protecting Providence, 50
Goombay Festival, 203–204
Gorrie, John, 153
Grand Floridian, 105
Graves, Michael, 105
Grayton Beach, 156
Great
— American Piano Competition, 206
— Explorations, 123
— Gulfcoast Arts Festival, 206
— Illuminations, 207

— Movie Ride, 102
Greatest Show on Earth, 132
Green Cove Springs, 190
Gregory House, 150
Gulf Breeze, 158—160
—Zoo, 160
Gulf Islands National Seashore, 158
Gumbo Limbo Nature Center, 204

— *H* —

Haas Museum Complex, 124
Hall of Fame, 193
Hard Rock Cafe, 110
Hatsume Spring Festival, 199
Haunted Mansion, 103
Hawkins, Captain John, 183
Hawthorne, 185, 194
Hearst, William Randolph, 71
Heliopolis, 113
Hemingway
— Days, 205
—Ernest, 90—91, 194, 205
—House and Museum, 90
Henry B. Plant Museum, 47
Henry M. Flagler Museum, 55—56
Heritage Park, 142
Hispanic Heritage Festival, 206
Historic Pensacola Village, 162
Historical Museum of South Florida
    and the Caribbean, 66
H.M.S. Looe, 89
Hobbies Magazine, 28
Hobe Sound, 31, 50—51
Hog Town, 195
Homassa Springs, 145
— Wildlife Park, 145
Homestead, 77—80
Hopkins Boarding House, 163
Hotel Ormond, 34
Housman, Jacob, 87
Hungarian Traditional Costumes, 35
Hurricane
— Memorial, 86

— Museum, 92
Hurston, Zora Neale, 196
Hutchinson Island, 31, 47. 49—50
Hyatt Regency Grand Cypress
    Hotel, 106

— *I* —

IllumiNations, 102—103, 204
Indian
— Key, 87—88
—— State Historical Site, 87
— River City, 45
— Shores, 143
— Summer Seafood Festival, 206
— Temple Mound Museum, 157
International
— Bok Carillon Festival, 202
— Harvester, 67
— Swimming Hall of Fame
    Aquatic Complex, Museum and
    Pool, 62
Islamorada, 86—87
Isle of Eight Flags Shrimp Festival,
    202
Isozaki, Arato, 105

— *J* —

Jacksonville, 16—20, 24, 171, 190,
    202, 204, 206
— Art Museum, 19
— Beach, 21
— Jazz Festival, 206
— Zoo, 17
Jefferson County Watermelon
    Festival, 204
Jensen Beach, 47
J. N. "Ding" Darling National
    Wildlife Refuge, 137—138
John and Mable Ringling Museum
    of Art, 129

Jonathan Dickinson State Park, 50—51
John F. Kennedy
— Memorial Torch of Friendship, 68
— Space Center, 43—45
John Gorrie Museum, 153
John Pennekamp Coral Reef State Park, 84
Jones, Lois Mailon, 119
Joscak, Joseph, 145
Julee Cottage Museum of Black History, 162
Junior Museum of Bay County, 155
Jupiter, 50, 52, 65
— Inlet, 31, 204
— Inlet Lighthouse, 52
Jungle Cruise, 103

— K —

Kapaha Botanical Gardens, 196
Kenan, Mary Lily, 55
Kennedy Space Center 43—45
Kentucky Derby, 192
Key
— Largo, 84
— West, 53, 82, 89—93, 177, 205
—— Aquarium, 92
—— Author's Room, 92
—— Lighthouse, 89
—— Museum, 92
Kidspace, 18
Kingsley
— Plantation State Historical Site, 15
Kingsley, Zephaniah, 15
Kissimmee, 95, 101, 107—108, 199
— Cow Camp, 114
Korenshanity, 139
Koreshan
— Unity, 139
— State Historic Site, 139, 202

— L —

Ladies Home Journal, 113
Lafayette Vineyards and Winery,176
Lake
— Buena Vista, 101—107, 204
— City, 189
— Jackson Indian Mounds State Archaeological Site, 174
— of Mayeime, 65
— Okeechobee, 65, 107
— Wales, 113, 202
— Weir, 100
Lakeland, 111, 118
Lalique, René, 97
Largo, 142—143
Lauderdale, Major William, 60
Laurelton Hall, 97
Lavalle House Museum, 162
Leedskalnin, Edward, 80
Leu
—Botanical Gardens, 96—97
—House Museum, 96—97
Lighthouse Museum, 29
Lightner
— Museum, 28
— Otto C., 28
Lincoln, President Abraham, 24
Lindberg, Anne Morrow, 138
Little
— Havana, 69, 201
— Talbot Island State Park, 15
Live Oak, 183—184
— Tree, 159
Loch Haven Park, 95—96
Loggerhead Sea Turtles, 47, 204
Longboat Key, 128
Longwood, 99
Looe Key National Marine Sanctuary, 88
Lowe Art Museum, 75
Lowry Park Zoo, 120
Lue Gim Gong, 100
Lunar Festival, 202

— M —

MacDonald, John D., 196
Maclay, Alfred B., 173
MacIntosh, John Houston,
Madison, 182
Magic Kingdom, 102—103
Maitland, 98—99
— Art Center, 98—99
Mallory Square, 93
Manatee, 146
—Village Historical Park, 126—127
Mandarin, 12, 30
Marathon, 88
Mangoes, 136
Marcos de Apalache State Historic Site, 176—179
Marianna, 168
Marie Selby Botanical Gardens, 131, 203
Marineland, 33
— of Florida, 33
Marjorie Kinnan Rawlings State Historic Site, 194
Marriott, Fred, 34
Masaryktown, 145, 203
Matanza River, 30, 33
Mayport, 16—17
— Ferry, 16
— Naval Station, 16—17
McGuire St. Patrick's Day Parade, 201
McLarty State Museum, 47
Medieval Fair, 201
Melbourne, 46
— Beach, 47
Mel Fisher's World of Treasure, 106
Memorial Presbyterian Church, 29
Menéndez de Aviles, Pedro, 25, 28, 30
Mercury Astronauts, 42, 44
Merrick, George, 73—75
Merritt Island, 43, 47
— National Wildlife Refuge, 43

Miami, 52—54, 64—69, 83, 201, 205–206
— Beach, 69—70, 198, 204
— Jazz Carnival, 204
— Marine Stadium, 69
— Metrozoo, 75
— Museum of Science and Space Transit Planetarium, 67
Micanopy, 193, 207
— Country Festival, 207
Milton, 167
— Imogene Theatre, 167
— Opera House
Mizner, Addison, 56, 58–59
Moccasin Lake Nature Center, 142
Model T Ford, 135
Monastery of St. Bernard, 71—72
Monroe, Commodore Ralph, 72—73
Monticello, 181, 204
Morikami, George Sukeji, 58
— Park, Museum, and Japanese Gardens, 58, 199
Mormon Church, 46
Morse, A. Reynolds and Eleanor, 123

Morse, Charles Hosmer, 97
— Museum of American Art, 97
Mote Marine Aquarium and Science Center, 131
Mount Dora, 100, 199
— Art Festival, 199
Mulberry, 112
Museum of
— African–American Art, 119
— Archaeology, 62
— Art, 62—63
— Arts and Sciences, 39
— Botany and the Arts, 131
— Commerce, 162
— Fine Arts, 123
— Florida History, 172,
— Historic Containers, 108
— History, 14
— Industry, 162
— Science and History, 18

— Science and Industry, 120
— Sea and Indian, 157
— Sponge Diving, 144—145
— Theater, 25

— N —

Naples, 139—140, 205
— Depot Civic and Cultural
   Center, 140
NASA
— Art Gallery, 44
— Spaceport USA, 43
National
— Hurricane Center, 74
— Lead Company, 22
— Museum of Naval Aviation, 164
Natural Bridge Battlefield Historic
   Site, 177, 200
Nature Center of Lee County and
   Planetarium, 136
Naval Live Oaks Park, 159
New Capitol, 172
New Smyrna Beach, 40—41
Noah's Ark, 150
Nolan, John, 132
Nombre de Dios, 28
North
— Florida Cracker Homestead
   Interpretive Center, 149
— Hill Preservation District, 162
— Miami, 71—72
— Port, 133
Norton Gallery of Art, 57

— O —

Ocala, 185, 192—193, 202, 205–
   206
Ocalifest, 205
Ocean Drive, 70
Offshore Reefs Archaeological
   District, 79

Old
— Capitol, 171
— Christ Church, 162
— City, 22, 25
— Cracker House Visitor Center,
   114
— *Folks at Home*, 188
— Ironsides, 159
— St. Johns County Jail, 29
Oldest
— House, Key West, 93
— House, St. Augustine, 25
— Store Museum, 26
— Wooden Schoolhouse, 27
Olmstead, Jr., Frederick Law, 113
Olustee, 189, 200
— Battle Festival, 200
— Battlefield, 189, 200
Open Boat, The, 41
Orange County Historical Museum,
   95—96
Orchid Festival Week, 203
Orlando, 94—97
— Museum of Art, 96
— Science Center and John
   Young Planetarium, 96
Ormond Beach, 33—36
— Union Church, 35
Osceola, 24
Overlook, 114
Overseas Highway, 83—84, 86, 88
Oysters, 152

— P —

Palatka, 190—191
Palm
— Beach, 50, 53, 55—57, 200
— Polo Club, 60
— Coast, 33—34
Palmetto Leaves, 30
Panama City, 155, 206
— Beach, 155

Park Avenue
— Historic District Downtown,
   Tallahassee, 173
— Winter Park, 97
Parrish, Maxfield, 97
Payne Mansion, 131
Paynes Prairie State Preserve, 197,
   202
Peacock, Isobelle and Charles, 72
Pee Dee River, 188
Pelican Island, 48
Pennekamp, John, 84
Penney
— Farms Memorial Community,
   190
— J.C., 190
Pensacola, 148, 161—164, 166, 171,
   201, 203, 206
— Bay, 158
— Historical Museum, 162
Pepper Creek, 145
Pepsi Manatee and Aquatic Center,
   120
Perkins, Maxwell, 194
Perry, 149
Pfeiffer, Annie, 111
Philip II, King of Spain, 30
Phosphate Museum, 112
Pier, St. Petersburg, 123
Pinellas County Historical Museum
   and Heritage Park, 142—143
Pirates of the Caribbean, 103
Plant
— City, 199
— Henry B., 111, 117, 122, 141
Pleasure Island, 104
Polish Fest, 206
Polo Clubs, 60
Ponce de León, 27, 40, 83, 166
— Inlet Lighthouse, 40
Ponce Inlet, 40
Ponte Vedra
— Beach, 21—22
— Lodge, 22
Pope, Dick, 115

Port
— of Miami, 68
— Orange, 40
— St. Joe, 153—154
Pratt, Captain Richard, 24
Psycho, 110
Putnam House, 190

— Q —

Queen Anne's Revenge, 85—86
Questor, 120
Quina House Museum, 162
Quincy, 168—169

— R —

Raccoons, 138
Ravine State Gardens, 191
Rawlings, Marjorie Kinnan, 185,
   194, 196
Reconstruction Period, 30
Rebel's Refuge, 187
Red Cross, 119
Remington, Frederic, 108, 118
Reptile World Serpentarium, 109
Restored Spanish Quarter, 25
Revolutionary War, 23—24
Ringling
— Brothers, 48
— Brothers and Barnum &Bailey
   Circus, 132
— Clown College,132—133
— John and Mable, 116, 125,
   128—129
— Museum of Art, 131, 201
River Bridge, 35
Robinson, Sam, 201
Rockefeller, John D., 26, 31, 34—36
Rocket Garden, 44
Rock Harbor, 84
Rogers, Will, 36
Rodes, Charles, 60

Rollins College, 97
Roosevelt, President Theodore, 48, 118
Roseate Spoonbill, 137
Rough Riders, 118
Royal Palm Polo Club, 60
Royal Poinciana Hotel, 55, 57
Ruins of the Sugar Mill, 126
Rubens, Peter Paul, 130

— S —

SR–71 Blackbird Reconnaisance Plane, 158
St.
— Augustine, 12, 22—29, 161, 201, 204, 207
— — Aquifer, 27
— — Beach, 29—30
— Cloud, 46, 101, 109
— Johns Lighthouse, 16
— — River, 12, 16, 20, 24, 190
— Joseph, 153
— Lucie's Inlet, 48
— Marks, 176, 178
— —Episcopal Church,191
— River, 177
— Mary's Church,190
— Nicholas Greek Orthodox Cathedral, 144
— Petersburg, 116—117, 122—124, 201
— — Historical Museum, 124
— — Shuffleboard Hall of Fame, 124
Salvador Dali Museum, 122—123
Sam Robinson Jazz Festival, 201
Sand Castle Contest, 205
Sanford, 99
— General Henry R., 99
Sanibel, 136—138, 201
— Stoop, 137

San Pedro, 88
— Underwater Archaeological Preserve, 88
San Simeon, 71
Sarasota, 125, 128—130, 201, 203
— Bay, 131
Satellites and You, 44
Saturn V, 43
Savage, Augusta, 190
Scenic Boat Trip, 98
Schribner's Magazine, 194
Schulze and Weaver, 57
Schweizer, Nils, 111
Sea
— Island Cotton, 15, 182
— Sea World of Florida, 109
Seafood Festival, 206
Seaside, 156
Sebastian Inlet, 47—48, 204
Sebring, 113, 200
— George, 113
— International Raceway, 200
Selby, Marie, 131, 203
Seminole Indians, 24, 60, 63, 73, 79, 86—88, 95, 140, 205
Seminole Indian Wars, 79, 182, 195
Senator, The, 99
Seven Mile Bridge, 88
Seville Historic District, 163
Shrimp Docks, 14
Siege of Pensacola, 151
Silver Spurs Rodeo, 199
Singing Pines, 59
Sistrunk Historical Festival, 199
Sky Over Jacksonville, 18
Smith, Jules Andre, 98
Smithsonian Institution, 144, 153
Snows of Kilimanjaro, The, 90
South
— Florida
— — Museum and Bishop Planetarium,127
— — Railroad, 111
— Miami, 75—76
— Ponte Vedra Beach, 21

— Seas Plantation , 138
Space Coast Science Center, 46
Space Mountain, 103
Spanish
— American War, 13, 118, 121
— Military Hospital, 27
— Night Watch, 204
SpectroMagic, 102—104
Spongeorama Exhibit Center, 144—145
Sports Hall of Fame, 189
Spring Bayou, 143
Springtime Tallahassee, 201
Standard Oil Co., 26, 34
Stanley Steamer, 32, 34
Star of David, 71
Stephen Foster State Folk Culture Center, 186—189, 203
Stephens, Robert, 169
Stern, Robert A. M., 105
Stetson University, 100
Stone, Edward Durrell, 108, 172
Stowe, Harriet Beecher, 12, 30
Stranahan House, 63
Sugar Mill Gardens, 40
Sumatra, 149—150
SummerFaire, 205
Suncoast Seabird Sanctuary, 143
Sunshine Skyway Bridge, 124
Survivors Camp, 47
Suwannee River, 185, 187
Suwannee Springs, 183
Swan Hotel, 105
Swinging Bridges, 191

— T —

T. T. Wentworth, Jr., Florida State Museum, 162
T–34 Fixed Wing Aircraft,167
Tallahassee, 165, 170—174, 201
— Jr. Museum, 173
— St. Marks Historic Railroad 176 179

Tampa, 116—122, 145, 198–199
— Bay Hotel, 117—118
— Museum of Art, 119
Tarpon Springs, 107, 143—145
Tanner, Henry, 119
Teach, Edward, 85
Team Disney, 105
Teed, Cyrus Reed, 139, 202
Tequesta, 51
— Indians, 62, 65
TH–57 Helicopter, 167
Their Eyes Were Watching God, 98
Tiffany, Louis Comfort, 28, 97
Titusville, 42, 206
To Have and Not Have, 90
Torreya State Park, 150
Trapper Nelson Interpretive Center, 51
Tupperware World Headquarters, 108
Tuscawilla Park Reserve, 39
Tuttle, Julia, 66
Typhoon Lagoon, 104

— U —

Uncle Tom's Cabin, 30
Underwater Demolition Team– SEAL Museum, 49
Universal Studios Florida, 110
University
— Library, Gainesville, 196
— of Tampa, 117
Upjohn, Richard, 191
U.S.
— Air Force, 142
— Air Force Armament Museum, 158
— Astronaut Hall of Fame, 42
— Corps of Engineers, 158
— Naval Air Station
— Mayport, 16—17
— Pensacola, 162—164, 202
— Navy Pirate Fleet, 83

— Space Camp, 42
USS
— Constitution, 159
— Forrestal, 16
— Saratoga, 16

— V —

Valpariso, 158
Vatikiosis, Sozon, 144
Venice, 132—133
— Arena, 132—133
Venetian Pool, 74
Vietnam War Veterans' Memorial,
    171
View from the Capitol, 171
Villazon and Co., 121
Vizcaya, 67
V. M. Ybor Cigar Factory, 122

— W —

Wakulla River, 178
Wakulla Springs, 177—178
Walt Disney World, 94, 101—105
Warm Mineral Springs and Cyclo-
    rama, 133
War of 1812, 149, 159
Washington Oaks State Gardens, 33
Water Ski Museum and Hall of
    Fame, 115
Weeks Air Museum, 76
Wentworth, T. T., Jr., 162
West
— Orange County, 101
— Palm Beach, 57—58
Whale and Dolphin Show, 109
Whitehall, 56
White Springs, 186—189
Whiting Field, 167
Wiggins Store, 127
Wild West Stunt Show, 110
William Bartram Day, 202

Williams, Esther, 115
Winter
— Fest and Boat Parade, 207
— Fantasy on the Waterway, 207
— Haven, 115, 199
— Park, 97—98
Winton, Andrew, 37
Wirick–Simmons House, 181
Wood, John A., 118
Woodville, 177, 201
World Showcase, 103
World War I, 86
World War II, 22, 49, 76, 108, 158
Worth Avenue, Palm Beach, 55
Wrecker's Museum, 93
Wright, Frank Lloyd, 94
Writers' Hall of Fame, 196

— XYZ —

Yacht and Beach Clubs, 105
Yamato Colony, 58
Ybor City, 118, 121, 198
— State Museum, 121
Yearling, The, 185, 194
Young, Owen D., 33
Yucatan Current, 156
Zellwood, 203
— Sweet Corn Festival, 203

Photographic Credits

Florida Department of Tourism: cover and pp. 13, 15, 27, 40, 41, 42, 48, 51, 52, 54, 56, 60, 64, 69, 70, 75, 82, 85, 89, 93, 94, 113, 122, 124, 126, 129, 130, 134, 137, 138, 141, 152, 156, 159, 170, 171, 175, 181, 192, 198

Florida Photography Archives, pp. 7, 20, 24, 26, 32, 32, 36, 59, 64, 66, 78, 81, 90, 91, 98, 106, 117, 118, 129, 135, 140, 144, 146, 151, 161, 163, 167, 168, 169, 179, 180, 182, 183, 184, 186, 188, 194, 195, 197,

Museum of Arts & Sciences, Daytona Beach, p. 39

Ringling Bros. And Barnum & Bailey Circus, pp. 128, 132

After Words

Thank you for the opportunity to share my favorite places with you. In an attempt to keep this guide current and helpful, your comments and suggestions are invited. We would also be grateful for information about your favorite places throughout Florida.

My comments are:

_____

_____

_____

_____

_____

_____

_____

☐ Check here if you would like to be added to our mailing list and please provide your name and address _____

_____

_____

Please mail to:

Tailored Tours Publications
Box 22861
Lake Buena Vista, Florida 32830

Additional copies of this guide may be purchased through your bookseller, or for $14.95 per copy (including tax, postage, and handling) from Tailored Tours Publications, Box 22861, Lake Buena Vista, Florida 32830.